JAPAN

AMERICA

My Journey: From Kobe, Japan to Hagerstown, Maryland

MASAHIRO HIRAI

CONTENTS

DEDICATION

Dear Kenji,

What a year 2014 has been to our family.

I'm sorry that you have had such a tough and hard time in your life, and I could not do anything for you. I really appreciate your positive thinking and bright reactions to everybody. You are a very strong person, and I am so proud of you. You always care for and are thoughtful to everyone, myself included. For just one example: do you remember when we went to the emergency room for the first time at Johns Hopkins Hospital? We stayed in a small room and waited for a doctor for quite a while. You asked the nurse, "please, can you bring a comfortable chair for my dad?" My tiredness is nothing compared to your pain, and yet you thought of me. How wonderful my son is!

Thank you.

When I think about you— your behavior, tastes, and personality—reminds me just of me when I was your age. We are very similar in many ways.

Maybe it would be interesting to you to know how I decided to come to the United States. I think that it is a very special case for one man to leave from his home country of Japan over 40 years ago without any special reasons. Normally, working men in Japan automatically stayed with their company until retirement (55 years old was typical retirement age at that time).

Now, I'll share the journey of my life with you.

Departure

September 14, 1974. 7:52pm.

Northwest Orient Airline Flight 58, destination Los Angeles via Honolulu, moved slowly away from the terminal building at Haneda International Airport in Tokyo. I was sitting by the small window of the plane and looking outside at the bright illuminations from the terminal building and the dark night sky. In one moment in my mind, I felt that I would never come back to this land and sky forever. Then, I heard the noisy engine start up and watched my hand gripping the arm rest begin shaking. I had flown many times before, but that night especially, the roar of the engine and strong vibration seemed to fill the entire cabin. A few seconds later, the pilot released the brake off the heavy body of the Boeing 707 and quickly gained speed on the narrow runway. Before I knew it, we were off the ground flying high into the night sky. I looked down the shimmering lights of Tokyo and admired its beauty and vibrancy. Narita Airport had not yet been built. So I left from Haneda Airport, which was only fifteen minutes away from the heart of Tokyo.

Soon the plane was high into the atmosphere, well above the cloud line in the sky. I could not see anything anymore from the window, only my face, wet from tears, in the reflection. I did not even cry when my father died. I was just eighteen years old then, but the tears never came. I did not know why I cried that night.

Maybe I felt that I was leaving my country forever, or maybe it was because I made my mom cry, feel sad, and be disappointed in my decision.

My mom, openly weeping, asked, "Why do you have to go America?" "Sorry mom, but this is my only opportunity to change my life," I said. It was the same response as it had been each time she asked over the past month. My brother was standing beside her, and he looked right at me but did not say anything. He knew that I would not change my mind.

Five months earlier, in April of 1974, my college friend, Kubo, called me. "Hirai kun, do you want to go to America?" He continued, "I just came back from Washington, DC. If you want, I can introduce you to a very special person. His name is Frank Ikard. He's the president of the American Petroleum Institute and is a former congressman from Texas." Kubo added, "He is looking for a young man to work at his house. I was there with Mr. and Mrs. Ikard for 3 years. The job is very easy, and Mr. Ikard will help you get a green card."

I was 27 years old, at that time. Since college graduation, I had spent five years working at the Hanshin Railroad Company like my father before me did. Ten people I knew from college joined me at the import cargo department. I spent three years there before transferring to the trading department, where I endured another two years of work. I did not like the job there.

There was absolutely no private life. There was no tolerance for individuals with unique abilities or ideas. Any suggestions for the company's improvement were rejected. Workers had to hide their faces and couldn't speak or socialize with one another. Workdays were six days a week from 9am-9pm, with half days on Saturdays. Then people would go to the bar with their boss and sometimes our customers. To me, that was no way to live. I wanted to spend my free time doing something I enjoyed. I imagined what my life would be like, ten or twenty years down the road, going through the motions day after day, with little challenge or room for advancement and no excitement or ability to cultivate a private life outside the company. If I stayed in Japan, I felt that my life was already programmed. I would live the same way for decades to come.

So I asked myself, *is it okay this way?* I knew the answer already. *No.* I may live another forty or fifty years more and do the exact same thing as other millions of guys do. I wanted to do something I really like, whether I was successful at it or not. I was searching for somewhere that has fresh air, green grass, blue skies, and a rolling sea. Just thinking about it, I felt free.

I knew in my gut that Kubo's offer was my way out of the repetitive, monotonous life ahead of me in Japan. This was the opportunity I had been waiting for. In July, after several letters exchanged between Mr. Ikard and me. I opened the mail to his latest letter from him—he was preparing a green card for me and expecting to see me soon.

Back in the steel body of the Boeing 707, Flight 58 had leveled out and was cruising at maximum altitude. Inside the cabin, people were beginning to relax from the bumpy start to the flight.

Some passengers got up to use the restroom, and others lit up their cigarettes. But I was still in tears.

The plane was at about 50% occupancy. Not many people took a plane overseas for their vacation, for even in 1970 it was very expensive to purchase a plane ticket. For a one way ticket from Tokyo to Washington, DC, I spent 175,000 yen. In American dollars, that would have been around $583.00. With inflation and the current exchange rate, that ticket would cost approximately $1750.00 dollars.

Japan to Hawaii is a seven hour flight. I had been asleep for an hour or two before I heard the cabin announcement: "This flight is now in the landing position at Honolulu International Airport. Please make sure to fasten your seatbelt and put your seat back to its original position. The no-smoking sign has been turned on."

I stopped at Hawaii because I was expecting to meet up with a friend, Tokiko Hashimoto. She used to be my contact person at Urashima Electric Corporation, which was one of my company's customers in Tokyo when I was working in the import trading section. At that time, the Japanese government controlled the import of computers and computer parts from the UNITED STATES to protect the Japanese computer industry. So, small businesses like Urashima had a very difficult time importing IC panels from the UNITED STATES During the two years I spent in the transfer department, I was responsible for helping import computer parts as sample items for Urashima and for handling quotes from my company to them, too. They really appreciated what I did for them, so they sometimes arranged special dinners for me. Urashima's higher officials, Tokiko being one of them, invited me to special nightclubs and restaurants once a month. Later, she began to join me at dinner alone. Tokiko and I became good friends.

In July, Tokiko told me, "I have to go to Hawaii." The owner of Urashima Electric established a sports fishing company in Hilo, Hawaii. Tokiko was to be the new company's manager. "So, please come to visit me in Hawaii," she said. I responded, "I may go to visit you in September because I'll be traveling to Washington, DC, for my future job." She was so surprised when I told her I was moving to the United States.

Flight 58 arrived at Honolulu International Airport on time at 9:45am. It was already hot outside of the terminal building, the sun torching my skin, but soon a cool breeze blew and I found shade under a nearby tree. For the next two hours, I waited for next Aloha Airline flight from Honolulu to Hilo, where Tokiko would be waiting for me. I remember sitting down on the bench in front of Gate 52, thinking *now is when I really start my new future*. I wasn't worried about anything.

A small aircraft, the Douglas DC-6, carried fifteen passengers from Honolulu to Hilo. This short-distance, lower altitude flight would take only forty-five minutes and also give passengers a chance to enjoy views of the nearby ships and the lush, green islands below. It was so beautiful! Arriving at Hilo, I was the third person to exit the plane. I walked down the stairs on to the black tarp walkway, and a special view was soon before me. Every way I turned my head, I saw the sparkling, emerald ocean and the lighter turquoise water of Hilo Bay. Colorful sailing and fishing boats floated on surface of the water. Tall coconut trees surrounded the one-story terminal building of Hilo Airport. I easily spotted Tokiko among the handful of people waiting for their flights just outside of the terminal building. She had on a bright yellow V-neck tee shirt and was waving and smiling at me. She had been there for only two months, but her skin was already tan. Her first words to me were, "Aloha from Hawaii." "Good to see you in Hawaii!" she said again, happily. I picked up my luggage from the towering luggage cart placed right beside the plane. Smaller, local airports such as this one often didn't have a designated place to check bags or a baggage claim area.

I took my luggage to her car, a 1968 Plymouth Fury. It was a two-door sedan with a 5.5 liter engine, which to me was impressive, for the average sedan in Japan then had only a 1.5 liter engine. The car cruised easily down the paved, black asphalt leading away from the airport. Tall coconut trees and volcanic rocks lined both sides of the road. It took only fifteen minutes to get Mrs. Urashima's house, which was on the middle of a hillside just outside the city of Hilo. Mrs. Urashima would be providing me housing during my time in Hawaii.

"How do you do? Welcome to Hawaii," Mrs. Urashima politely greeted me. She was a very gentle-looking, tall, slender woman in her forties. "Please enjoy your stay with us," she said, smiling at Tokiko. "Thank you for letting me stay," I responded. Then, she showed me to my room. I stayed there for three days and two nights. My room was downstairs, but it felt just like the first floor because the way the house was built into the slope of the mountain. From my window, I could see all of Hilo Bay.

After I rested a little bit and took a shower, I went upstairs and sat down in Mrs. Urashima's comfortable living room chair and looked out at Hilo Bay. My eyes still felt heavy. I might have drifted back to sleep until I was surprised by Mrs. Urashima's voice coming from in front of me. "Isn't it so beautiful from here to the Bay? We were very lucky to get this house," Mrs. Urashima said before sitting down beside me. "Also, we might be able to open our sports fishing business quickly, too," she continued. "Would you like to go fishing with our new boat tomorrow?"

"That's wonderful! Thank you!" I loudly answered, thrilled with the idea. I loved the sea and had small sailing boat with a friend back in Tokyo.

Urashima's fishing boat was quite large, maybe more than 70-80 feet long. The bearded captain, likely in his sixties, welcomed me to the ship. We spent three hours cruising that day with no other vessels on the ocean horizon. There were so many fish moving about under the sea, visible through the glass plate on the ship's floor.

Afterward, Tokiko took me to a beautiful black-sand beach near the Mauna Kea volcano. By the time she took me to a restaurant in Hilo Marina later that night, I already wished I could stay here rather than go on to Washington, DC. I had never been this comfortable and relaxed before in my life. As if she read my mind, Tokiko offered, "If you want to stay here, I could get you a job and place to live." "I have to go Washington. Mr. Ikard is expecting to see me," I told her confidently, but deep down, my desire was to just stay in Hawaii.

Made from Scratch: A Recipe for the American Dream

WASHINGTON, DC AND SHEPHERDSTOWN

I arrived at Dulles International Airport at 5:05pm, on Sept 17, 1974. It was my first time visiting Washington, DC, and I wasn't feeling particularly excited or joyful. Then, again, I wasn't feeling depressed or worried either. I just felt calm and unemotional. Herman Patterson, Mr. Ikard's personal chauffeur, was 27 years old, the same as me. He was waiting for me at the luggage area. He just walked straight up to me and asked, "are you Japanese? "Yes, I am. Are you here for Mr. Ikard?" I asked him. He smiled and nodded his head. "I'm glad you speak a little English."

Herman drove me back from the airport in a Cadillac Fleetwood limousine, which quietly came to a stop at the front entrance of the Shoeham Americana Hotel, one of Washington's oldest hotels on the corner of Connecticut Avenue and Calvert Street. I was surprised Mr. & Mrs. Ikard lived in a hotel. We walked into the large lobby area filled with tourists and employees of many races. I felt that I arrived in Washington, DC, and entered different world because I saw there were many people who looked different from me. Herman opened the door of Room 412, and said very loudly, "Mr. and Mrs. Ikard, the Japanese boy is here." Mr. and Mrs. Ikard quickly entered the entrance hall with nice smiles.

Mr. Ikard was a towering man, standing at 6'2" and over 250 lbs. He wore round glasses and had a kind-looking face. "I'm Mr. Ikard and this is my wife, Mrs. Ikard. We're glad to see you," he said. Mrs. Ikard, a small women with green eyes, freckles, and long red hair, turned towards me. "I'm Mrs. Ikard. Welcome to Washington. You must be very tired from your long travels, so please rest for a few days. Okay?" she asked. "Sorry, I wish I could talk with you more, but we have to go to the ball at the Kennedy Center now. So please excuse us and just relax tonight. We'll talk more with you tomorrow."

Twenty minutes later, I was alone in the Ikard's residence. Mr. and Mrs. Ikard, who did not know anything about me, still felt comfortable to leave me here alone. A special feeling came over me. Here I was, alone in America! I walked around their house and thought to myself: *what a very special first experience in the UNITED STATES.* I wondered what kind of guidance Mr. Ikard had for me or what job I would be doing for him, but for now, there was nothing. I could see the Capitol Building and the Washington Monument, some of the world's most important places, from the window of my room. I laid down on the bed, looked up at the ceiling, and a realization drifted into my mind. *I am in America, not in Japan.* Somehow, I wasn't worried about what the future held.

The next day, I found myself in the middle of a large, open field in America's capital city. People called this stretch of grassy land between the Capitol Building and the Lincoln Memorial "The Mall", though it wasn't like any mall I had ever seen. In front of me, I could see the entrance to the Smithsonian Air and Space Museum. I remembered Mrs. Ikard asking, "Massey, why don't you go to the Smithsonian?" I did not know what the Smithsonian was. I walked around many museum buildings such as National Gallery of Art, the Natural History Museum, and the Museum of Technology. I had never visited any museums in Japan before. I don't know why. Maybe they were too busy? Maybe I was not interested in them when I was younger, or maybe I just didn't have any time for myself. In any case, when I stood there gazing at eighteenth century paintings and the Wright Brother's airplane and real moon rocks, I had a strange feeling come over me. I realized more strongly than before that I was not in Japan. I felt further away then I was, even on the opposite side of the Earth. I knew on that day my life had taken a different direction. It was my second day in Washington, DC, and I felt like a newborn baby. I didn't have anybody I knew, no relatives, and I could barely speak or understand English.

Then I walked a long way, from Downtown DC to the Lincoln Memorial, stopped to look at the Kennedy Center, which to me looked like a square box-style castle, past The Watergate Hotel, and took M Street to Georgetown. I had never been to a European country, but I felt that Georgetown was just like one of old European towns I read about in books. There were tiny coffee shops, bars, restaurants and delicatessens, gift shops, art galleries, and grocery stores. The streets were narrow, cobblestone paths. To me, I felt that I had been transported to a toy-like town. I quickly became a lover of this Georgetown.

"Hello, Mr. Ikard! I'm back," I said as I finally made it back to Room 412. "What happened? It is already 7:00pm," came Mrs. Ikard's loud voice. Her eyes were wide and she had a surprised look on her face. "Is it too late, Mrs. Ikard? "I asked. "Yes, I thought you'd come home before 5:00pm! Anyway, it's okay. I was just worried about you." She turned and walked quickly back towards their room. I felt bad and had a sinking feeling in my stomach. She did not say anything to me about what time I supposed be back. I just stood there, alone, in the entrance hall for a while, feeling down. *I am 27 years old already, a pretty mature age. I know common sense. She spoke to me like she was screaming to a little kid,* I thought to myself. *If you want to me come earlier, you should tell me what time I should be home*. But I knew I should be careful. *There are so many different kinds of people here, and in Japan too*, I reminded myself. Also, in America everything is different. I didn't know any Japanese-speaking people here, only English-speaking people, and I didn't know the thoughts or customs of American people. Maybe my future here would not be as easy as I originally thought.

✦ ✦ ✦

Another morning soon thereafter, at around nine o'clock am, I heard my name being shouted from down the hall. "Massy!"Mrs. Ikard loudly called for me. "Yes, Mrs. Ikard. I will be back before 5:00pm today," I said quickly, before she had a chance to say something else. "No, no Massy, we have to go to New York today and will be back tomorrow afternoon. So, you can rest one more day here, and then we're going to West Virginia." "Am I going to go to West Virginia, too?" I asked. "Well, yes. We have a farm there. So from tomorrow, you'll stay there at our farm. It is a very nice place, and you will like it there." She didn't wait for me to answer and returned once more to her room. I left the living room, my mind racing. I thought I was going to be able to stay in Washington, DC, to help them clean their rooms and garden their little porch. I wanted to try to do something for my future in my spare time. I thought that maybe Mr. Ikard was testing me to see what kind of person I was or my quality and commitment to work. *This might be my chance to work towards a better job with a green card.* If I was in his position, I might do the same thing. I'd have to check out what kind of person was working for me. Anyway, I knew I didn't have much choice but to go with them.

While they were out, I left their home to go sightseeing again in Georgetown. I spotted a very nice coffee shop on M Street the day before called Cafe de Paris, so I went there.

Inside, I heard Salvatore Adamo's tune "Sans toi ma mie" playing, which was very popular in Japan a few years back. Young waitresses wore jeans with white tee-shirts and seemed to enjoy making conversation with the customers and going about their tasks. It felt familiar and reminded me of an old Japanese coffee shop where I used to go. It made me feel like I was back in Japan. I stayed about two hours and then took a walk near Georgetown University. Just blocks away from Wisconsin Avenue, there are many quiet, old places. I could see old railroad tracks. I wondered if they were from a street train that made stops in the city many years ago.

The maple tree leaves softly hit my face while I walked, and I looked up to see where they fell from and realized that the season must be changing. They were no longer green and had turned to brilliant shades of yellow and burnt orange. I shivered as a breeze blew past me, and for some reason, I thought about Hawaii. For a few minutes in my mind, I was back on the black-sand beach, under the coconut tree. The gentle sea breeze washed over my face and I felt the tropical, Hawaiian sun. It was a very nice short vacation in Hawaii. The chill returned, and I kept walking.

✦ ✦ ✦

"This is the place," Mrs. Ikard said that Friday afternoon. Mr. and Mrs. Ikard had brought me to their farm near Shepherdstown, West Virginia. I got out of Mr. Ikard's Cadillac Fleetwood right in front of an old, white, wooden farmhouse. "Is this the house I'll live in now?" I asked, looking to Mr. and Mrs. Ikard for confirmation. They both smiled at me. Mr. Ikard said, "Yeah, go on in. All the rooms are still okay, and you can use any room you want to."

The house was two stories high, with four bedrooms on the second floor, one large primary bedroom, two living rooms, a library, and the kitchen on the first floor, and a game room with a pool table downstairs. I chose the smallest bedroom on the second floor, the one right above the kitchen. There was another small stairway that led from the kitchen to that small room. When I shared my room selection with Mr. Ikard, he nodded. "That's good." I knew that small room may be used be for their maid, but I did not say anything.

Their house was a one mile drive from the old farmhouse. The mountaintops of the Blue Ridge Parkway were visible from the top of the hill on their 500 acre farm property. The house looked quite new, with all natural stone covering each side of the home. It was a two-story stone building with two bedrooms on the second floor, the kitchen, dining room, and a huge living room on the ground floor, and a sauna and extra storage downstairs. Around the back of the house was a large swimming pool and a two-bedroom guest house.

As evening came, I helped them make dinner in the kitchen. They looked very happy to be preparing a home-cooked meal. *They must be tired of having restaurant meals and party foods during the weekday,* I thought. I wore a white jacket they had gotten me back in DC and served them their drinks and meals when they were ready. They went to the dining room and sat down. They taught me how to set a dinner table and how to serve drinks and meals in a very formal way. While they had their dinner, I had to eat dinner myself in a corner of the kitchen. I ate my meal quickly at the small kitchen table. I really felt down doing this job.

There are approximately four job status levels in Japan:

1. High-ranking political jobs, commercial land property owners, and owners of large, long-established companies.

2. Doctors and successful business owners.

3. Upper management in bigger companies, schoolteachers, and small business owners.

4. Salespeople, small merchants, and salaried employees. Servers, bartenders, blue-collar workers, and workers paid by the day.

In my mind, I had gone from the third tier status down to the fourth, so I could not possibly let my mom and brother know what I did.

"Massy," Mrs. Ikard called to me. When I went into the dining room, she smiled at me pleasantly. "Massy, you did such a good job! We are expecting our good friend to come visit us next weekend. Can you do the same next week as you were able to do for us today?" "Thank you, Mrs. Ikard. Sure, I'll do my best," I told her sincerely. "The guests that are coming next week are very special friends. Their name is Mr. and Mrs. Marychester. Mrs. Marychester's brother is the comedian Bob Hope. Do you know Bob Hope? Anyway," she continued, "from now on you will stay here and work the farm job during the week. On Monday morning, Woody, our farm manager, will tell you what to do, okay? Then you can help us here at the new farm. Sometimes we do not come down here, so you just take off and make yourself comfortable." I kept listening. She added, "And we will pay you $40.00 every week. You don't need any food, we won't charge rent, you don't need anything really, plus, you can make a call back to Japan once a month. Is that okay?" I couldn't really think of what to say or how I felt about their offer, so I just said "thank you" to Mr. and Mrs. Ikard.

After they left on Sunday afternoon, I slumped down into the wing back chair at the old farmhouse living room. *How could they make my payroll only $40 per a week? I was making $80 per a day in Japan until three weeks ago.* I just asked myself *why, why would Mr. and Mrs. Ikard make that decision? Did they think so little of me? They are multi-millionaires. To them, $40 dollars is nothing.* Of course, I did not come to the United States just for money, but it is too little. *What could I* *possibly do or say? Nothing.* Then, determination rose up in me. No matter how much I'd earn, I would work hard and let them consider whether a salary of forty dollars a week was fair for me or not.

The sun was still up, and I walked around the outside of the old farmhouse. I noticed the beauty of the home and land here, the white painted wooden fence all around the house, the rows and rows of apple and peach tree gardens, the old, red barn just a short walk from the house. There were two old, green tractors beside another work building. To the right of the house, there was small smoke house with blackened doorways.

There was a roughly 30 x 50 yard fenced pigpen near the barn, with about twenty hogs running around, squealing, and playing. What a different world this was. *Maybe this will be alright, fun even.* I never went to a countryside in Japan. I walked up the hillside behind the house and looked over the mountains and shadowy valleys during sunset. Something rose inside me, the beauty of it all. When the sun continued to sink into the horizon line and darkness began to fall, I went back to sit in the living room. The house was completely silent. No radio, no television. Just silence. I felt wet tears drip down my cheeks as I watched the remnants of the sunset out of the living room window. I had cried many times since I left Japan.

I never had experienced this much quiet time. Watching that sunset, I realized I would be starting my new life from scratch. I was starting at zero.

"Hey!" a rough, loud voice woke me with a startle. It was only 7:30am. I quickly changed clothes and went down to the kitchen. A large, looming man in working clothes stood near the kitchen door with sharp, strong eyes and a solemn face. "Hurry up! Time to get to work," he said, gesturing towards the door. When I got there, another man was waiting for me, sitting on top of a tractor. He signaled for me to go up to the tractor.

Later, I found out the first person who came to the house was Woody, the Ikard's farm manager. The person who would be working with me, the man on the tractor, is Jack. He looked about forty years old, with a short, stocky build. I tried making conversation with Jack, but I soon found out he is a very quiet person. I could tell there wasn't going to be a lot of conversation between us. The farm work was very challenging, rigorous work. The days started promptly at 7:30am and we ended at 4:00pm, with one thirty minute lunch break. At noon, I would quickly fix my lunch and eat. After our shifts ended at 4:00pm, I took a shower, for my body was dripping with sweat and dirt. Watching the sunset became part of my evening routine; I would walk up the hill, sit down on the grass, and gaze at the Blue Ridge Mountains and the orange glow of the setting sun.

On Friday afternoon once our work ended for the day, Woody gave Jack and me our paychecks. Jack got $80 (minimum wage $2.00 x 40 hours), and I would get my $40.00. Inside, Mrs. Ikard was waiting for me. "Massy, did you have a nice week?" "Sure, everything is good and new for me, so time goes by quickly," I responded, looking down. I did not say I was exhausted from the full week of hard manual labor.

On Saturday morning, when the Ikard's were expecting their friends to come visit them, I cleaned the dining room and living room and tidied up the guest house. Mr. and Mrs. Ikard were busy preparing a special dinner: pot roast and a fresh garden salad with rainbow trout. Everything they prepared came from their property. The beef was from one of their cattle. The vegetables from the garden were hand-picked. Jack and I fished at pond on their farm for the trout. The Ikard's raised hundreds of fish in their pond.

At 5:00pm on Saturday evening, the guests arrived at the new farm. I was busy serving cocktails. Most of the guests drank white wine and ate a lot of cheese. Six guests were enjoying talking with each other and Mr. and Mrs. Ikard. They gave their friends a tour around a farm and showed them the mountain view. Then, their friends sat down on deck chairs near the pool and in front of guest house where they would stay overnight and continued chatting and sipping their wine.

"What is that!?" Mr. Ikard suddenly exclaimed, speaking to himself when he came into the kitchen to check his pot roast. "What happened, Frank?" Mrs. Ikard came over and looked at him. "I think I've made a mistake. I might have put sugar instead of salt on the roast. Oh yeah, this pot roast is far too sweet. We cannot serve this!" "Oh my god! What are we going to do?" Mrs. Ikard asked, her voice high with worry. Her eyes were wide. "How much time do we have? They are getting hungry and are just about ready for dinner. Oh my GOSH!" Mr. Ikard screamed, and then stopped and looked over at me standing there. "Massy, do you think you can make some Japanese dishes? This is really an emergency," he asked, hopeful. I was shocked. I looked back at Mr. Ikard's face and saw his desperation. "Okay," I said tentatively. "I'll try."

I don't know why I said that. I liked cooking, but I never had any experience working at a restaurant. Also, the time and materials were quite limited. I thought quickly, considering my options. *I have to use that pot roast meat.* Fortunately, the meat was still tender. I washed the meat with running water to get the sugary glaze off and cubed the meat into small pieces. I grabbed a pan and sautéed the meat with fresh vegetables, added tomato sauce and a bit of soy sauce, and seasoned the dish well with a lot of fresh parsley and fresh spices. The whole dish was finished in under twenty minutes.

The guests and Mr. and Mrs. Ikard were already siting down in the dining groom having another round of cocktails. I served the salad and appetizers first. I heard Mrs. Ikard explain to the guests how everything they were eating had come from their farmland. Then I served the main course, wondering what they would think about it. "Mmmm! Oh wow, Massy! This tastes just like a delicious beef stew!" Mrs. Ikard said loudly to me from her seat at the table. "Oh my god! Did you make this? You are better than my chef!" Mrs. Marychester looked at me and said. "Massy, Mrs. Marychester owns a very famous French restaurant in Georgetown, "Mr. Ikard said. They continued the meal, chewing happily. When the dinner was over, the guests went to guest house. Mr. Ikard came and found me, looking relieved. "Thank you Massy, you are wonderful. You really helped out a lot tonight." He shook my hand and when doing so, pressed a fifty dollar bill into my hand.

Another week started. Jack and I were tasked with cleaning the inside of the barn. So, from Monday to Friday, we made hay into bales. It was very time consuming and very hard work. We stuck the bale of hay on to the wagon from the hay field, we had to move the the wagon to the barn, and finally we carried the heavy bales of hay into the barn.

By Friday afternoon, I could hardly walk upstairs. My legs felt like lead and my back was screaming in pain. Around 6:00 pm at night, Mr. Ikard came to pick me up so I could help them in the kitchen at the new farm. Mrs. Ikard was waiting for me when I arrived. "Massy, we have more guests coming tomorrow. So, can you make some dishes? We got very nice, fresh chicken from the Georgetown market," Mrs. Ikard asked. I paused a second before responding. "I can make some, but if I have some Japanese ingredients, I can make better food. Can I can get them the next time I go to DC?" "I understand. Just tell me what you need. I'll ask Herman to get them," Mr. Ikard said. So Herman got the ingredients, and the following night I broiled two chickens. When they were cooked, I sliced the chicken over a fresh vegetable bed, and drizzled them with a sweet ponzu sauce (we didn't have yuzu, so I used lime). Another success. The guests really enjoyed my dinner, and Mr. and Mrs. Ikard looked so pleased.

Before I knew it, another week started. We had to make bales of hay again. Woody told Jack and I that we had to get all the hay in the barn by the end of the following week. Woody showed up in the mornings and gave us our orders for the day, and then he disappeared the rest of the day. Sometimes I wondered what he did. Woody was like Jack. Unless he was telling us what to do, he didn't say much.

When I was Japan, I practiced judo and played baseball in high school and college. I was pretty strong, more than an average young person I guess, but this kind of work was grueling, even for people in the best of shape. I remember standing at the bottom of the stairs, one hand on the railing, looking up. I couldn't bring myself to climb them. *Another night of sleeping in the living room.*

Fortunately, Mr. and Mrs. Ikard were not coming to the new farm that weekend. On Saturday morning, I shoved all my dirty clothes into my bag and walked to Shepherdstown, about five miles away. When I got into town, I went directly to the laundromat. It was my first time using a laundry machine, but an older woman washing her clothes nearby must have sensed my confusion, came over, and showed me how to wash my clothes. I put fifty cents into the machine and then decided to go window shopping during the hour or more it would take to wash all my clothes.

Shepherdstown was small and quaint. The entire downtown was only two or three blocks long. I walked around for a few minutes before realizing that it was a college town. Through the trees I could see Shepherd College: several modern class buildings, and a nice, green football stadium that sat on the top of a hill beside the Potomac River. I was sitting down on a bench on the other side of street and was able to look down the street at both the regal college campus and also to the wooden bridge over the Potomac. It was beautiful and peaceful. My mind began to drift. I wondered about how all my friends in Japan were doing, especially the friends who used to go drink and talk with me after our jobs at a pub or restaurant. I wondered what they thought about their own futures and whether they had found happiness. I thought about Tokiko in Hawaii. *How different it is between her new exciting job managing the new sports fishing company and my job now, doing nothing special.* How she must be enjoying the perfect weather, the endless blue sky, and ocean in Hawaii. *I really miss Hawaii.*

I was so disappointed in my job here and the lack of money, but I didn't know what else to do other than to keep going. *If I left Mr. and Mrs. Ikard now, what would happen? Where would I go?* I didn't have any status, so I couldn't do anything. I couldn't find a legal job or get my own place to live. But I couldn't go back to Japan and admit failure. For me, the bottom line was that at least I had a comfortable place to stay and food to eat.

I took all my clean laundry and walked all the way back to the old farm. The door creaked open, and I went into the dark house. The big, empty house was always so quiet. There was still no radio or television in the house. I collapsed into the now familiar armchair, closed my eyes, and thought about the two months I had spent here, working hard on the farm through the week and preparing meals for the Ikard's on the weekends. Suddenly, I thought about the date. It was October 17th, and it was my 28th birthday. It was the first birthday I spent alone, with nobody around to celebrate with and nothing to do. Just then, the phone rang. "Hello, Masa bon?" It was mom's voice. "Is everything okay? Happy birthday!" "Everything is fine. I'm busy and am enjoying it here, so don't worry," I told her, trying to keep my voice from breaking. I couldn't explain how I was actually doing.

✦✦✦

A month later, in mid-November, Mrs. Ikard called. "Massy, next week, we will be there on Wednesday," Mrs. Ikard told me. I didn't know that the American Thanksgiving Day was approaching. The following Thursday morning, I was busy helping haul the Ikard's visitor's luggage into my old house. The guests included Mrs. Ikard's son, Bryan, and Mr. Ikard's son, Bill, and his wife Lisa. Bryan was a good-looking twenty two years old with blond hair. He was a student at the University of Texas. Bill, like me, was twenty eight years old and lived in Houston, Texas. Like his half-brother, he was tall and good-looking. He was a successful lawyer, and his wife Lisa was quite beautiful. She was homecoming queen their senior year at the University of Texas and was crowned Miss Texas in 1969. Now she was an up and coming supermodel. When I finished with the luggage and arrived at new farm, another car had just pulled up. It was Mr. Ikard's first son, Frank, his wife Carol, and their two children. Mr. and Mrs. Ikard were inside, busy preparing a large meal. "Massy, we are going to eat dinner at 3:00pm, okay?" Mrs. Ikard announced. I checked the clock, which read 10:00am. *Why are you rushing?* I wondered. *There is plenty of time.*

However, the time went by quickly. I carried around dishes upon dishes and was constantly filling up drinks. American people's ability to eat and drink, I noticed, far exceeded Japanese standards. The whole day, they just continued to drink and munch on hors d'oeuvres. I carved a whole, home-baked, country ham and put slices on a large platter in the middle of their kitchen. The twenty-five pound ham was almost gone by 2:00pm. At 3:00pm, the dinner table was full of other delicious foods: baked turkey, what was left of the ham, pork chops, five different kinds of vegetables, and a seafood dish I made. They continued to eat, drink, and enjoy until late that evening, around 8:00pm.

I quickly learned that Thanksgiving was an important holiday for American families. It appeared to be tradition for adult children to bring their families and go back home to their parents' house to get together and enjoy a meal for the Thanksgiving holiday. The Ikard's children stayed until Sunday and had a very good time.

After the Thanksgiving holiday, people started to decorate their homes for Christmas. The Ikard residence was no different. I helped to decorate both the new and old farms. *If we had snow*, I mused, *this farm would look just like one of those traditional Christmas cards.* Mr. and Mrs. Ikard were so busy in Washington, they stayed away from the farm for nearly three weeks. I stayed by myself at the old farm on the weekends. When I had extra time, I would go into Shepherdstown to visit the library at Shepherd College or go downtown and eat at Betty's restaurant. There were seemingly no other Asian men in the whole town, just me. So, I became pretty familiar to the town locals. "Hey, Massy!" they would greet me when I came by.

I continued my walks up the familiar hill behind the old farm, sit down and look around. If I looked far to my right, I could see a small island on the Potomac River. To my left, there was a small country road and the farm entrance with the white wooden fence. I could just make out Mrs. Ikard's special, hand-painted sign posted beside the mailbox that read "Island Green Farm." There were rarely cars or people that came down the country road in front of the old farm. Most of the time, I was the only person around as far as my eyes could see. My most enjoyable parts of the day included checking the mail, hoping I would receive correspondence from Japan or Hawaii. Usually, the mailman would deliver items to the mailbox just before noon. My best time was reading letters during my thirty minute lunch break.

Before I knew it, it was December 31st, 1974. Mr. and Mrs. Ikard did not come to the farm. I drank some beer and enjoyed some cheese in the evening and recalled New Year's Eve last year; it was a crazy night. My friends and I had partied the past two or three days straight. We drove up to the top of Mount Rokko and looked down over the city lights of Kobe's busy downtown area before going back down to a private property for a countdown party. I had so much to drink that the rest of the night was blurry. When I woke up, I was at somebody's bedroom with four other guys, all passed out in different spots of the room. It was nearly noon, and I had woken up with a throbbing headache. What a difference one year can make. Here I was, alone, on a five hundred acre country farm in West Virginia.

The first week of January 1975, I went to Washington DC with Mr. and Mrs. Ikard. There were a couple reasons to go to DC. First, we were to discuss changing my status (I still only had a visitor's visa). I also was to help move Mr. and Mrs. Ikard's residence to their new townhouse called Kalorama Square near DuPont Circle, so they didn't have to stay in the hotel any longer when they were in the city. "Massy, we have a problem with your paperwork," Mr. Ikard stated plainly. "We cannot change your visitor's visa to a working visa. I'm sorry. I still want you to stay with us," he added. I was shocked. *I could not stay America any longer.* My visa was to expire by middle of March. I never thought I'd have to worry about my status here. It was the basic minimum condition to be able to come to America and work. I just believed Mr. Ikard when he had assured me that it was no problem. After all, he was a former Congressman, a judge, president of the American Petroleum Institute, and a very rich man. It was my mistake to not double check and make sure that I had all the documents that would legally protect me. "Mr. Ikard, let me think about what I'll have to do from now on," I said sharply. It was all I could say. I don't know if he felt badly or not. When I got back to the old farm, I felt so down. For my status, I knew the best way was to obtain a permanent visa, but getting one was not easy. Changing from a visitor's visa to another kind of visa wasn't easy either. Maybe it would be possible to get a student visa. Going to school might be my only option for keeping a legal status in the UNITED STATES Considering the little time I had before my visa expired, I knew I'd have to take action right away.

In the meantime, I kept working on the farm. Manager Woody always had plenty of jobs for me to do, so I kept busy and was always tired.

One Saturday morning, I walked from the old farm to Shepherdstown. It was a nice day. To my right side I could hear the roar of the Potomac River and on the left-hand side there were six or seven well-kept houses. An old truck pulled out from one of the houses and passed me before suddenly stopping and backing up to where I stood. "Hey! Do you need a ride?" yelled a friendly-looking middle aged man. I looked at him. His window was down and he stuck his head out towards me, smiling. "Are you Japanese?" he asked. "Yes, I am. Thank you," I said and climbed up into the passenger's side seat. After I sat down, the truck got up to speed, and the man told me," You know, I went to Japan many years ago. Maybe before you were born." "When did you go?" I asked. "During the Korean war," he said, and extended one hand to mine for a hearty handshake. "Yeah, I was already born then," I replied. "I was about four or five years old." "Really? You look young," he said, continuing to drive. "What do you do here?" "I work at Island Green Farm for Mr. Ikard," I told him. "Oh, I know Mr. Ikard, but he does not know me," he said, joking. He winked at me. "I am Ward. What is your name?" "My name is Hirai, but Mrs. Ikard called me Massy, so you can call me Massy, too." "Okay, Massy," he said. "Maybe someday, you can come to my house. I have five children." I thanked him for the offer. *He was a nice guy*, I thought. *He sure was talkative.* Five minutes later, we were already in town. It usually took me forty-five minutes to walk one-way, if I kept up a pretty good pace. I thanked him again and hopped out of the truck. I did my grocery shopping and did my laundry at the coin laundromat. I took a walk through campus at Shepherd College and stopped for lunch at a small American restaurant before slowly heading back to the old farmhouse. I had a lot of food to cook up for dinner because Mr. Ikard had an account at a German grocery store. I could just sign and get anything I needed.

Later, I cracked open a beer and was thinking about what I would fix for myself when the telephone rang. It was Ward, the man in the truck I had met just that morning. "Massy, would you like to come my house now for dinner?" he asked. His house was very small. There were only three bedrooms with seven people living there. Everyone in Ward's family was very welcoming and very bright. His eight-year-old daughter Julie was especially cute. Everyone was so nice and made conversation with me. They wanted to know all about Japan, the food, customs, and what schools were like. It was the first time that I felt relaxed in the UNITED STATES For dinner, Ward's wife Mary prepared local, country food. I really enjoyed the meal and the company.

Made from Scratch: A Recipe for the American Dream

College Student

Two weeks after, I went to Washington to visit the Ikard's. It wasn't long before the topic of my status came up again. "Massy, what will you do about your status? Can you extend the visitor's visa another six months?" Mrs. Ikard inquired. *Why didn't you prepare for my status before I left Japan? You invited me to come to the UNITED STATES, but didn't think about how I would stay here?"* I replied in my heart. I really felt disappointed they did not care more deeply for me after how hard I had been working for them.

After trying every way I could think to extend my stay, it came down to the student visa option, which meant that I would have to become a student again. I was thinking a little about Hawaii because Tokiko still wrote to me and asked me come back to Hawaii. She thought it would be easy for me to get a job, but I wasn't so sure. I couldn't go back to Hawaii without a job, and there was no way that I could return to Japan, either. I didn't want to feel like a loser. I knew I couldn't go backwards. It had been four months since I first arrived, and I was determined to continue pressing forward. I would have to see whether I could exchange my visitor's visa for a student visa.

I shared my plan with the Ikard's the next time I went to Washington. "Mr. and Mrs. Ikard, I think it's better to try and get a student visa, so I'm going to try and go back to school." They smiled and said, "That's a good idea! Since we are moving to the townhouse, we will prepare a nice room for you. If you could go to school here in DC, you can stay with us and help out some in the evening and on weekends, so you don't have to stay in West Virginia," Mrs. Ikard offered. I was very busy when I got back to the old farm. I had to contact my college administration office and college professors in Japan for my records and recommendations. I also studied every chance I had in preparation for the college entrance tests. I was not sure I wanted to go back to college or would get admitted. I was already twenty eight years old and never thought I'd be back in school again.

In March, I took all the documents and my college application and visited the Admission's office at George Washington University. In April, I got letter from their office which said: "We are pleased to admit you to the Masters of Business Administration program at George Washington University. However, it is too late to join the class that begins this September. You will begin classes during the Spring semester of January 1976." It was very good news, but I was disappointed I could not go in September. I knew this meant that I might have a problem to legally stay in the UNITED STATES until January.

I went to Washington several times that April. My room at Ikard's new residence was downstairs but had a nice, large window, which brought in plenty of natural light and offered a direct view of the Capitol Building. "Do you like your room, Massy?" Mrs. Ikard asked me. "Yes, I like it very much," I told her truthfully. "Also, it only takes me about fifteen minutes to walk to GW from here." She beamed, and replied, "Good! I talked with Mr. Ikard about your school. He said we can help pay the tuition for the fall semester at Georgetown University, just to study English. That way, you can get your student visa from Georgetown University too, and then from January continue with your program at George Washington." *They were thinking about my status, too!* I never thought about going to another school in the meantime. I accepted the offer and thanked her. I felt like they did care about me staying. Plus, she was right. I did need to study English, too.

But there was more news. "We will be leaving soon for summer vacation at Martha's Vineyard, Massy," Mrs. Ikard continued. "It is a beautiful island. You'll like it!" Mrs. Ikard said to me. "Martha's Vineyard? Where is it? I have to go, too?" I asked. "In the state of Massachusetts," she replied. "And yes, you'll go, too." Even though I was so happy about my school situation, I didn't understand why they were always making decisions about where I'd go without asking about my feelings or opinions. *I am just an object to them. Do they even think of me as a human being?* Maybe they did care for me some, but maybe it was only because I was useful to them.

Towards the end of April, I was in my room at their townhouse when I heard someone knock at the door. When I opened the door, there were three huge, muscular men standing there. They flashed me their identification cards, and said sternly, "We are federal agents, and we have to inspect your room." I felt my face turn red and I stood very still, my knees locked in place. I thought I submitted everything to extend my visa the previous month, but I had not yet gotten my approval letter. *Oh my god! They've come to take me back to Japan.* I felt sick to my stomach. However, they moved past me without saying a word and quietly checked through the items on my desk and in my closet. After about ten minutes, which felt much longer than that, they said, "thank you" and left, closing the door behind them. I had no idea what was going on.

I went upstairs and asked Mrs. Ikard what had happened. "Massy, they are Secretary of State Kissinger's secret police. They have to check out anywhere he will go beforehand for security measures. See? They are upstairs now, checking things out there, too," Mrs. Ikard said reassuringly. "Tonight, we are hosting a big party and there are a number of important people coming here," she explained. "Massy, you don't have to do anything tonight. We already prepared to have a special catering company come, and they do everything. There will be musicians, too!" "Shall I help you?" I asked her. "No, no. This will be a black-tie cocktail party, very formal, so you just stay in your room," she said. "Oh, well maybe you can help to open the door when guests begin to arrive," she added after a moment's thought. So, I wore my white jacket and stood by the door.

At 7:00pm, the doorbell started ringing continuously and well-dressed people came, one couple after another. I recognized some of them from the television: Senators Brooke, Stone, Bentsen, and Goldwater, Mr. Walter Cronkite, Mr. James Reston, Mr. Ted Coppel, and even Barbara Walters! The guests stood around in circles talking enthusiastically with one another. Some were dancing, and others had gone out to the patio and looked like they were holding a private meeting.

I thought about how different this American party was compared to a Japanese event. Everyone here was acting individually, there was not one person who was conducting the whole party and there was no toast. Couples seemed to leave after about two hours or so, whenever they wanted to, I guess, without any announcement or direction. I could tell that the most important guest was the Secretary of State, Henry Kissinger, so when he left, people seemed to lose interest and slowly trickled out of the room. He had an extra armed car behind him when he left and a mass of people following him in their cars and on the street.

✦✦✦

Mrs. Ikard was right. It was a beautiful place, that Martha's Vineyard. We had arrived that Saturday afternoon during the Memorial Day holiday, on May 30, 1975. We left Washington DC early that morning around 7:00am. The drive was about nine hours; we got on Interstate 95, and then from Woods Hole, we took a ferry from the port at Vineyard Haven to Martha's Vineyard.

The whole island exuded New England style. The town had plenty of small houses: some were wooden, some brick, and many of them had front yards outlined with white picket fences. Around the gates, roses and many other fragrant flowers were blooming. Almost all the houses had flower boxes hanging below the windows, full of brilliant, red geraniums. There were no franchise stores such as McDonalds, Burger King, or Kentucky Fried Chicken. People used bicycles to go everywhere. There were only three screens at the movie theatre. I went to one of the showings to see the new movie, *Jaws*, which had been filmed in Martha's Vineyard the previous summer. It was my first experience going to a movie theater in America. The Ikard's house was in Edgartown, which was on the southeast side of the island, or what the locals referred to as "downisland." The house had its own beach at the edge of Edgartown Bay. Nearby, a small ferry boat (that could carry only two cars) allowed travel to Chappaquiddick Island where Senator Edward Kennedy had his car accident scandal in 1969.

I had a busy daily schedule. At 8:00am when my days began, I was to go to the general store to pick up a newspaper for Mr. and Mrs. Ikard. I'd come back and spend several hours helping to clean their room and living room. After that, I'd have free time until 5:00pm. In the evenings, I would help prepare dinners or parties, and when they went out, I'd be free until the next day.

In my free time, I would go to the beach to fish or swim or do nothing at all. Sometimes, I would ride my bike to the other side of the island. My favorite place was the small fishing village called Menemsha, meaning "still water." Menemsha had a narrow but deep bay and an old, historic harbor where many fishing boats would park. Rows of New England-style houses lined the harbor. Some houses had tiny, fenced porches on their rooftops, used to watch schools of sardine or mackerel come in from deeper water. About one mile off the coast from Menemsha lies the Gulf Stream, which runs from Florida to Canada carrying large schools of fish and the whales that follow them.

One afternoon in the middle of June, the Ikard's hosted a big party in their backyard. "Massy, you'll see an interesting dinner tonight called a clam bake," Mrs. Ikard said. There were over fifty people crowded into the ½ acre backyard, enjoying their cocktails and appetizers. Bob and his helper, who were there to bake the clams, arrived late, and they were just starting to prepare the gas steam system and dinner table. The dinner was supposed start at 7:00pm, but at 6:30pm, nothing was even close to being ready. All that was there was a huge steamer sitting on top of a large gas burner. Thirty minutes later, right on time, a blaring horn sounded. And Bob and his helper quickly dumped trays upon trays on to the tabletop. Each tray was piled high with clams, shrimp, lobsters, chicken, sausage, many other vegetables. All their guests came to the table and helped themselves to what they wanted. I was used to watching dinner and all sorts of parties, but this is style, to me, was wild. One of their guests was opera singer, Barbara Siles. "Massy, Barbara Siles is a famous singer, but her daughter is deaf. She never will hear her mom's beautiful voice, isn't that terrible?" Mrs. Ikard confided in me later.

Later that summer, during the month of August, movie star Lorne Greene and his wife, Nancy, came to stay with us. They were such good people, especially Mr. Greene. He was polite and was able to make conversation with just about anyone. He was one of the most popular actors at the time, and everybody knew him. But, he didn't ignore people like many celebrities do, and he was quite friendly with everyone. He liked to walk to downtown Edgartown in the mornings, and in the afternoons, he would often sit on a comfortable wingback chair in the living room and read a novel or science book. One afternoon, he asked whether I wanted to go to the ice-cream shop with him.

When we went there, so many people came up to him and said something, and every time, he would nicely respond to their comments or questions. I was so glad to experience a different part of this beautiful America at Martha's Vineyard during the summertime.

✦✦✦

By September 1975, I had become kind of excited to attend an American school. I was taking only English for international students at Georgetown University. Once school began, I thought less and less about Hawaii or Japan. Both my daily schedule and environment had changed quite a bit in the time that I had been here in America, from working on a farm and living by myself in West Virginia to starting school at a university and enjoying life in Washington. Each day, I would walk from Kalorama Square, located on 21st Street and take S Street to Georgetown University.

From S Street, it was a nice, straight twenty-five minute walk to the main gate of Georgetown University. The class I was taking was only for international students. I thought the class would be large, but it was small class with only twenty students. I was one of two Japanese students, and there were three Korean students, three Turkish students, two Libyan students, five Arabic students, three Iranian students, and the rest from other countries around the world. I was very hungry to meet and speak with other Japanese people, for I had not spoken my native language in over a year. The other Japanese student was called Ishihara, who was around my age. I didn't know it then, but we would go on to know each other all our lives. It was funny—I quickly realized that it was so much easier to understand each other when we, foreigners, talked together. It felt so much better than talking with native English speakers.

One day, when Ishihara and I sat down on a bench at one of Georgetown University's cozy gardens, an Asian-looking guy came and asked us, "are you Japanese?" "Yes, we are," I told him. "I'm Morita! Welcome to Georgetown," he said. Morita was a slim guy with long hair and had a brightly-colored, long muffler hanging from his shoulder. He smiled at us. "Nice. You can join our Japanese society; we have a meeting next week," he quickly explained. He was so cool that I thought he was a movie star, but somebody told me later that he was the son of Sony CEO and Founder, Morita Akio. No wonder all the audio systems, TV's, and computer systems were Sony products at Georgetown University. English class was easy, only three or four hours from Monday to Friday. I was starting to feel more comfortable in daily life and felt like I was on my way to a better tomorrow.

Before I knew it, it was Thanksgiving time again. The Ikard family gathered all together for the first time at Kalorama Square. Kalorama Square was comprised of two townhouse buildings and large garden space and swimming pool between them. Each building was four stories high and contained ten separate units. The Ikard's house was the first home on a corner, which had the most space. My room downstairs was near the garage door, and we were always using the garage. There was also a bathroom and laundry room on the lower level. On the first floor was the kitchen, dining room, living room, and garden. The second floor had a library and large living room for parties, the third floor had the Ikard's bedroom and living room suite. The fourth floor had two guest bedrooms. The townhouse had its own elevator. Outside the elevator hung an expensive painting, which Mrs. Ikard bought from an artist at Martha's Vineyard. Sometimes I didn't understand why they spent money on items that were so unnecessary.

In came Frank and Carol with their three children, Bill and Lisa, and Bryan. Frank and Carol's family was large, so they stayed at the Washington Hilton Hotel, which was only two blocks away. I was more comfortable taking care of the family's holiday dinner than I was the year before. This second year on American soil felt easier, and I was physically and mentally much more adjusted to this way of life.

One day after Thanksgiving, I was invited to a party by my English class classmates who was from the United Arab Emirates and was one of the King's sons. When I arrived, I was so surprised. The party was being held at the famous The Watergate Hotel and the dinner was unlike any I had attended before. They did not use any dinner table or chairs. There were many Saudi Arabian people wearing traditional thawabs and evening wear. Many different mouthwatering dishes were served on the floor. Ishihara and I enjoyed the party immensely and marveled at their riches and customs that were so different from ours.

After Thanksgiving, the city once again got ready for the Christmas season. I enjoyed my walks from Kalorama Square to Georgetown University every morning. Kalorama Square is at the corner of 18th Street and T Street. I walked two blocks to Massachusetts Avenue, which is in front of the Canadian Embassy, and then I kept going. When I got to the bridge that passes across Rock Creek Park, I looked down and saw cars moving beside the nearby stream and kept going on Massachusetts Avenue for another two blocks. On my left-hand side I passed the British Embassy and saw the Gabon Embassy to my right. Three or four blocks away stood the Iranian Embassy on right and the Vice President's residence to the left. There are so many countries embassy's on Massachusetts Avenue that people sometimes call it Embassy Road.

As I walked, I remembered that Elizabeth Taylor and the Iranian Ambassador came to the Ikard's residence for one of their parties. This particular ambassador was a relative to Iranian King Shah. Mr. Ikard's organization (the American Petroleum Institute) had a business relationship with the country of Iran. So when King Shah's wife, Farah, came to the United

States, Mr. and Mrs. Ikard sometimes spent time with the Iranian royal family. I saw the pictures of when they went to Aspen, Colorado together with Elizabeth Taylor.

Anyway, I passed the bridge over Rock Creek Park and turned left just before the British Embassy, headed towards S Street. This was a quiet residential stretch, only one block away from DC's main streets. Almost every window of these homes had Christmas decorations and nice candles. I walked another three blocks before I hit busy Wisconsin Avenue in Georgetown. I still liked Georgetown best; one of the big reasons was that it just stayed in a classic old-fashioned way, with smaller specialty stores and shops. Like Martha's Vineyard, there weren't any franchise stores in Georgetown. I passed a few small delicatessens and grocery stores just off Wisconsin Avenue. Once, I saw an older couple setting out vegetables and fruits in front of their store. Their hard work gave me extra energy to get through the day. Georgetown University is only three blocks from Wisconsin Avenue.

After my class in the afternoon, I sometimes stop by a pub called The Tombs just near the front of my class building. Downstairs from the University shop there was another American restaurant called 1789, and it was equally as delicious. As far as I know, they are both still in operation today. Most of the time, though, I would just go back to Kalorama Square and help Mrs. Ikard. I knew the month of December was very busy for Mr. and Mrs. Ikard. They went to plenty of holiday parties and prepared their own party at home. So, I was busy too. One morning near Christmas time, Mrs. Ikard called me loudly from the kitchen. "Massy, come up and watch TV with me." I went upstairs. "Today is Barbara's last *Today Show* on NBC. She is moving to ABC," she said. I knew from the newspaper that Barbara Walters got a three million dollar contract with ABC. "I know, Mrs. Ikard, it is big news. How about Mr. Walters?" I asked. She smiled and said "Massy, you know!?" I smiled and said, "Yes, I know Senator Brooks." Barbara came to Ikard farm in Shepherdstown many times. In the beginning, Mrs. Ikard introduced me to Mr. and Mrs. Walters. But Mr. Walters did not exist. Barbara Walters was single. The man came with Barbara was Senator Edward Brooks. It was almost time for the presidential election, and President Ford was selecting a running mate. Senator Edward Brooks was a one of the candidates, but finally he picked Senator Dole. I liked Senator Brooks. He is very kind and spoke the same way regardless of who he was talking to. When he spoke to me, I could tell he was listening and trying to understand me.

"Happy New Year, Mother!" I told my mom over the phone. "Happy New Year, son. I'm so glad you called me. How is everything?" She sounded happy to hear my voice. "Yes, I'm fine." "I've been worried about you, but I feel like you sound a little bit better than last year," she said, clearly relieved. I think that every mom would have heard the difference in my voice between last year and this year. "Mom, I will start to go to college again from next week," I told her. "Why? You already went to college here," mom asked. I didn't explain in detail that it was necessary for me to go. "Anyway," she added. "Going to school is always good." My American life was better, yes, but I still felt like I couldn't tell my mom exactly what I had been doing here. But, I got off the phone feeling comfortable since mom thought I was okay.

Finally, it was January 1976, and I could begin my studies at George Washington University. There are two rival schools in Washington DC. I went to both schools. There were so many differences between them. Georgetown University was more of a typical college campus. Don't get me wrong, it was a very nice college campus, with a lot of greenery (trees and gardens) and some playing fields for baseball and football. But George

Washington didn't have any of those features. I felt like GW was more of a business-style place. Maybe that's just because I was in graduate school now, taking business courses. Anyway, it felt fresh and different to be on a new campus. GW was even closer from Kalorama Square than Georgetown, about a fifteen minute walk. There wasn't much of a student center or gathering area, so students would often socialize at the Marvin Center, which had a cafeteria and large lobby space.

I made new friends, most of them with international backgrounds: Japanese, Korean, Chinese, Iranian, Indian, and Thai. Many of them came from very special families too, just like my friends at Georgetown. This time, though, I met many more Japanese students. My friend Tsuchiyama was taking political science courses and quickly became a lifelong friend. Ando was taking MBA courses like myself and had been a baseball player at Waseda University, one of the best private universities in Japan. One of his teammates was Okada, who became a star player for the Hanshin Tigers, which was my company's team, and he drove a BMW. Many of my other new friends also drove fancy, well-known car brands. Tokunaga was the son of the family-owned furniture manufacturing company had a Porsche 911SC. Kaneko, son of a famous Arita artist, drove an Alfa Romeo. Sanada was a son of a twelve-generation sake company, had a Mercedes 632 coupe. Kobayashi, son of a yakuza leader (Japanese mafia), had an Alfa Romeo Spider. Nobuchi was son of large construction company in Kyushu and drove a Corvette. Only Tsuchiyama and I did not have cars.

I remembered that my former boss, Mr. Miyoshi, was promoted to be the president of the Hanshin Tigers a few months ago. I decided to write him a letter. I wrote: *I have been in the United States now over one year. The time has gone by so quickly. Thank you for allowing me to work with you in Japan. So far, I'm doing fine, and I am attending school again. I met Ando, who is a team friend of Okada at Waseda*

University. He has joined your team now. I don't miss Japan too much, but I do miss watching the Hanshin Tigers play.

Two or three weeks passed before a letter came in the mail. He sent a letter back to me that read: *Thank you for your letter. I am glad you are doing well in the United States. I talked to Okada, and he said that Ando was the captain of the team now and is a good player. If you have a chance to visit Japan, please come see me at the Tigers spring camp at Aki, a small city of southern part of Japan.*

The first thing I did after reading his letter was to call my mother. "Mom! My former boss, Mr. Miyoshi, is now the president of Hanshin Tigers, and he sent a letter to me and invited me to go to the Tigers spring camp," I told her, excitedly. "Mom, you can go with Yo chan (my brother)." "Really, we can go?" She was surprised. She had been a fan of the Hanshin Tigers for a long time. Her husband, my father, was employed until the day he died. He had heavy stroke when he was on the way home one day, fell into a coma for ten days, and died at only 48 years old. Her father-in-law, my grandpa, also was employed until retirement, and Yo chan and I worked, too. I really hoped Mom would have a special time at the Tigers spring camp. I felt sorry for my mom. I was not a good son and was selfish for thinking only of myself in my decision to come to the United States without her and my brother.

Author's note:

Kenji passed away at 5:30 pm on July 20, 2017. I was supposed to continue my story for Kenji, but I just could not pay attention to my story because of Kenji's illness. From 2015, his condition became much more serious. I just forgot that I wrote this document for Kenji.

Today is January 10th, 2020. I'm sorry I didn't get a chance to share this story with you, Kenji. I really wanted to tell you who I was long ago and how I finally settled down in Hagerstown. Kenji, your body has gone from this world, but I believe your soul is still here with me always. I know you'll be with me as I continue to write my story about you and our family and House of Kobe until now. So, I should continue my story for completion. I may show this to your brother Seiji, and sister Maki, and Mom, and to my five grandkids, too. I'll let them know how I came to the United States and how I settled my foundation in Hagerstown. Is it okay, Kenji?

Back in 1976, I felt that starting at George Washington would give me a fresh start.

"Hirai san, why don't we go to New York to play baseball? I know one guy who was a bar owner there, and he has a team now," one of the Japanese students told me when we got together one evening at the pub in Georgetown, Café de Paris. My friends always called me "Hirai san" because I was the only one five-seven years older than them. In Japan, even a person just a few years older would be respected by those younger than them by adding the phrase "san" after the family name rather than using a first name or nickname. My friends Ando and Tokunaga would often go to New York to drink at Japanese restaurants and bars— and to drive around in Tokunaga's Porsche 911SC. These Japanese students were all from very rich families.

During Spring Break, all the Japanese students left Washington, DC for to play baseball in New York. We took by 4 cars: the Porsche, an Alfa Romeo, a Corvette, and a BMW. It was my first time visiting New York City. Tokunaga told us, "There is a traffic signal right after the Lincoln Tunnel. If you stop at the signal, many teenagers will come over to your car window. Make sure you give them five dollars, okay? If you don't, they'll scratch your car."

While we were driving to New York, I thought about what a different lifestyle I was living now compared to my life in Japan two years earlier. I found myself wondering whether it was okay to have this much fun without seriously trying for my future. But once we got on the New Jersey turnpike, Tokunaga interrupted my thoughts and asked me, "Hirai san, do you want to drive my car for a while?"

"Yeah, sure," I told her. "Just a little. I've never driven this kind of super car," I said. So I drove the Porsche 911sc with its 6 cylinder air cooling engine. If I stayed in Japan, I never would have had this kind of opportunity. As we passed the Newark Airport on the left side, the highway became so wide, at least 10 lanes per side. I 'd never seen such a huge, busy road before in my life. While I was still taken back by the size of the roads before me, I saw many skyscrapers over the Hudson river out of my right hand window. *It must be New York City, the biggest city in the world.* I saw the Empire State Building with my own eyes. What a sight it was!

We came to Mr. Iwasaki's bar, which was on the ground floor of an old hotel building near Central Park. "Tokken, (Tokunaga's nickname) you really came!" Mr. Iwasaki, overjoyed, came over to us as soon as he spotted us in the bar. The bar was small and dark, and it had one old, wooden countertop that could seat ten– fifteen people. "Mr. Iwasaki, tomorrow's game is between New York and Washington," Tokunaga told him. "Yes, our team is excited for tomorrow. You don't have to stay here late. I already have two big rooms upstairs," he said. I guessed that Tokunaga came often and stayed in the hotel above bar. We went to our room on the 15th floor. From our window, I saw bright lights on every building. The whole city was alive, moving. *I am in New York!*

"How was the baseball game, Massy? Did you win?" Mrs. Ikard asked me when I came back to Kalorama Square on Sunday. "Yes, of course we won! It was so nice to see New York

City, Mrs. Ikard," I told her, smiling. She had been so nice to me and given me a lot of extra free time since I moved from Shepherdstown to Washington. My job was only an hour or two of light cleaning every day, mostly the living room and kitchen. I also continued to make dinner for Mr. and Mrs. Ikard at home and make dinner at their friends' house two or three times a month.

During my free time, I would spend time at GW or go to restaurants with friends. We would often go to a new sushi restaurant that had opened near Georgetown called Sushi Ko, which was the first sushi bar in Washington DC. I spent the most of my pay at Sushi Ko. The owner of Sushi Ko, Mr. Inoue, believed me to be a very rich student. Sometimes I would go there myself and just sit at the sushi bar and talk with the chef. One night when I was there, Mr. Inoue quietly asked me, "Hirai san, would you move to the table?" "Why do I have to move to the table?" I asked. He bent down and whispered quietly to me, "Congressman Yamanaka just came here." I slowly turned around and looked near the door. Two men were standing there and looked back at me. I recognized one of the men from tv. He was about 40 years old and had silver metal framed glasses. When I moved to the small table near the door, I looked at him and the shining gold badge on the collar of his black suit. It was the same symbol that each Congressman put on their jacket collar: a chrysanthemum design similar to the Emperor family seal. Congressman had a free transportation pass. All they had to do was just show their gold badge. He just ignored me and slowly went to the sushi bar without saying a word.

A couple days later, when I went to Sushi Ko, Mr. Inoue told me, "Hirai san, I'm sorry for the other night when I asked you to move tables. Many Japanese Congressman are difficult; they are far too proud about their position." "Inoue san, it's okay. No problem," I assured him. While I was having sushi, I heard Mr. Inoue's voice say, "Mr. Minata, please come sit beside this young man." When I looked towards the door, I saw a skinny man in his forties begin to walk towards me.

He came and sat down next to me. "Hi!" he said. I said hi back to him and asked "Are you Japanese? Your name is Japanese." "I'm American, but I'm also 4th generation Japanese," he replied. We talked a lot about Japan and America and food. He was very friendly and spoke a bit of Japanese, too. "Do you like America?" he asked me. "Yes, I do." He nodded, smiling. Still curious, he asked, "What will you do after your studies at GW?" "I hope I get a job here and am able to stay a long time in the US," I answered him. Another week, when I went to Sushi Ko, Mr. Inoue told me that Mr. Mineta was a Congressman from California. "Oh wow, the American and Japanese congressmen that ate here were so different in the way they treated people," I told Mr. Inoue. "Hirai san, it's not only him." Mr. Inoue added, "there are more Japanese congressmen like Congressman Yamanaka. They think they are in a special elite class." I was so surprised that Mr. Mineta spoke to me kindly and with interest. He didn't flaunt his position or speak down to me. He just enjoyed speaking about our common interests like two equals.

✦ ✦ ✦

In early May 1976, I got a phone call from Japan. "Aniki (Brother)! Mother fell down the steps three days ago, and she is in intensive care unit. Can you come home quickly?" Youichi said. I was shocked. Only a few days before this phone call, I received a letter from mother which said she had a very nice time visiting the Hanshin Tigers' spring training camp. I shared with Mrs. Ikard about what had happened and she told me, looking concerned, "you should go see your Mom."

It had been only two years since my flight from Japan, but I felt so different standing there at the Narita Airport. I felt like I was visiting other country. But that familiar feeling of home washed back over me while I was in the shinkansen (the

Japanese bullet train). I looked out at the rice fields submerged in water and the vegetable fields growing in dark, rich soil. People were working out in the fields. These were my people. *Yes, this is the Japan I know.* Over the fields in the background, I saw the majestic white peak of Mt. Fuji. As soon as the train pulled into Kobe, I went directly to the hospital, worried about the condition mother might be in. Mom had already moved to a normal room with three other patients. "Masa bon!" She recognized me. Her face lit up. Her color was good, but she had trouble standing up by herself. I was so relieved after seeing her smiling face. "Arigato," she said, thanking me. "I had a very good time at the Hanshin Tigers spring training camp. I met many players and Mr. Miyoshi, their president." Her voice was happy and she hadn't stopped smiling. I knew she felt good that I had come back to Japan. I was glad I had come back, for my mother and also for myself. I stayed in Japan and visited for three weeks, savoring the time. I met and caught up with old friends and spent most of my time keeping mom company. She was discharged from the hospital a week after I arrived.

I left Japan at the end of May from Northwest Airlines via Anchorage for Washington, DC. Despite the nice visit, my mind was full of worries. I had to drop all of my classes for Spring semester. It was not easy because of the time too late. Generally, at GW, students could only drop classes during the first four weeks of the semester, but they were able to make an exception for me because of a family emergency. In addition, I was feeling troubled by my financial situation. I had gotten my own car in April before I got the phone call about my mom's fall and spent $2,500 for a 1972 Ford Gran Torino full size station wagon. A month later, I spent another $2,000 for the trip to Japan. It was an expense I had not accounted for. On the other hand, I was excited to drive my own car to Martha's Vineyard. Mrs. Ikard told me, "Massy, when you come back to DC, can you drive yourself to Martha's Vineyard? We might be gone for the summer by the time you get back." So, I planned to meet them there.

The flight landed in Anchorage, Alaska to fill up the gas tank and to do an immigration check. "Mr.! You cannot enter this country," an immigration officer shouted at me as I got off the flight and shared my information. I was embarrassed and couldn't meet his eyes. "Your student visa is expired," he barked. "I am still going to school, George Washington University," I tried to explain. "No, your visa was for Georgetown University." Suddenly I realized that I got an I-94 form from GWU, but I forgot to go to the immigration office in DC to make the change. "Officer, I'm sorry. I made a mistake," I acknowledged. "I simply forgot to take my I-94 form to the immigration office and have my information updated. I have American family who supports me during the school year. Would you please call them in DC?" He ignored me and stared at me for a second with an unpleasant face and just said, "follow me."

The officer took me to his office and checked all my luggage and went through all my personal things and my pants pockets. I only had seven hundred dollars cash. I had to provide a phone number for Mr. and Mrs. Ikard and show my student ID from GWU. While I was waiting, an airline officer came and asked the immigration officer, "how's everything going in here? The plane has already been delayed an hour and the passengers are becoming agitated. "Just hold the plane for a while longer. We're contacting someone in DC," the immigration office said firmly. The call finally went through. Mr. and Mrs. Ikard must have vouched for me because the sour-faced officer took me back to the plane. Once we got to the gate, he turned and left without saying a word. I walked down the jetway, climbed into the airplane, and found my seat. The other passengers stared at me as I walked by. "We are very late because of you!" one woman seethed under her breath, just loud enough for me to hear. Everyone looked so angry, and I felt my face get warm.

"Mrs. Ikard, I'm sorry I made trouble for you last night," I told her on the telephone as soon as the plane landed in DC. She and Mr. Ikard had already gone to Martha's Vineyard. "Massy!" she breathed into the phone, exasperated. I could just picture her face, her eyes burrowed and lips pinched tightly. "In the future, please be careful. Legal status is very important in America," she chided me. "You will be very busy today. You will have to go to GWU and get another I-94 form, and then go to Senator Kennedy's office. The secretary will give you the paperwork, and then go to the Immigration office to meet the director," she continued to rattle on. Mrs. Ikard was a very emotional person. She was easy to get angry but also easily pleased. I knew by now that she wasn't angry with me, just flustered with the situation and worried about my ability to stay in the US. "Thank you, Mrs. Ikard. I'll take care of this problem right away," I told her.

That day was the first time I went to Senator. Edward Kennedy's office. When I opened the large, heavy wooden door to his office, I was greeted by a polite and fair-looking young woman who introduced herself as his receptionist. "May I help you?" she asked. "Yes, I am Massy Hirai from Mr. and Mrs. Ikard. I was told Senator Kennedy would have a letter for me about my immigration situation," I explained. "Please, follow me," she said and escorted me to another large room. There were three more beautiful women in the next room who smiled to me. One of them, a tall brunette, stood up and shook me hand. She told me quietly, "I talked with Mrs. Ikard yesterday," and gave me the envelope. She added, "The Senator is on the phone right now but he said good luck!" I could not see Senator Kennedy, but I still felt relieved because Mrs. Ikard made arrangements for me with her friend, and now I had the paperwork I needed.

"Senator Kennedy said he knows you and you are a nice man," the hefty immigration director said, folding the Senator's letter back up and sticking it in a yellow manila file folder on his desk. "Everything looks good from our end. We will update the information for your school visa." I had never met Senator Kennedy, but he wrote a letter for me. I felt a huge weight lift from my shoulders. "Thank you very much, and everything is okay now thanks to you, Mrs. Ikard," I told her when I got back to Kalamora Square.

I left Washington the next morning at 6:00am for Martha's Vineyard. My full-sized car made it easy to enjoy the drive with cruise control. At the time, it was a newer technology. I didn't even have to keep my foot on the pedal and was still able to go 65 mph consistently for most of the ride.

I arrived at the harbor to catch a ferry to Martha's Vineyard at around 6pm. 45 minutes later and I was bound for Vineyard Haven. The sun was still high in the sky. The days were getting longer as we approached summer. I sat down on one of the hard ferry chairs and watched the seagulls swoop down from the air trying to catch the other passengers' food. Even though Martha's Vineyard island wasn't far from the mainland, I didn't see any land. It was just the deep blue water and some fishing boats pulling in loads of fish. That evening, there was a warm ocean breeze. I inhaled deeply and felt the salty air in my nostrils.

I remembered when the ferry pulled into Vineyard Haven that it would be another 30 minutes to the Ikard's house in Edgartown. My stay was off to an early start the next morning. Usually the Ikards would stay in the family room in the mornings to leisurely read the paper or watch tv. Just as I had done the summer before, I would get up early to get them their morning paper and sometimes coffee or milk at the general store on the corner of Water St. and Main St. The store was even used as a filming location for *Jaws*. Sometimes I would enjoy taking a look around before returning with the morning paper. There were so many goods to peer at: assortments of candies, rows of ice cream tubs, freshly-sliced deli beats, fresh produce misted regularly, and even a hardware and sporting goods section.

"From tomorrow we will have many friends stay with us, Massy," Mrs. Ikard said. "It's going to get pretty busy for you." They weren't kidding. There was a steady stream of guests and parties all summer. Mr. and Mrs. Orrisman, who owned seven car dealerships, stayed for a week. As soon as they had gone, Mr. and Mrs. Lorne Green stayed for two weeks. Mr. Green was as personable as ever. Mr. and Mrs. Bradshow, the owner of an oil company in Texas came to stay the week after that. It felt like I was always cleaning up, preparing for dinner parties, and helping the guests with whatever they needed.

It was indeed a very busy summer in Martha's Vineyard, but unlike last summer, I had my own car and was able to see more of the island and enjoy what free time I had. I would just get in my car and explore the island. I'd go to so many nearby towns: Menemsha, Chilmark, Chappaquiddick Island, Gay Head, and Oak Bulf. Each town had its own unique landmarks and specialty stores. It was the last week in August when the Ikard's and I returned back to Washington. My classes at GW were about to begin again. It was about that time when I noticed that we had a major gas shortage. I remembered that when my friends and I went to New York City just before spring, it was not easy to get gas, even in New Jersey. Many gas stations had limited quantities of gas for sale. Some stations offered only ten gallons for each customer, and some gas stations closed altogether. In turn, the price of gas spiked; that year, it had tripled in cost, from 50 cents a gallon to $1.50 a gallon. Washington, DC was no exception; every gas station had long lines of people waiting for gas. Mr. Ikard was busy because of his position as president of American Petroleum Institute. Sometimes major television stations came to their house Kalorama Square hoping for an interview.

I knew I would soon be busy with school and work, but Mr. and Mrs. Ikard were also very busy due to the presidential election that year. I thought that Senator Edward Kennedy could be a presidential candidate, but he did not try. If he had, he would have likely been backed by the Democratic party. In preparation for the election season, Mr. and Mrs. Ikard had a full calendar of social events. In the last week of September, they had a massive party at Kalorama Square. Some of the guests I was familiar with by now, like Barbara Walters, Walter Cronkite, Ted Kappel, and Corky Robinson. I noticed that Barbara Walters did not come with Senator Edward Brooks. "Mrs. Ikard, Senator Brooks did not come with Barbara Walters this time," I noticed out loud, hoping she would know something. "Yes, they are no longer together," Mrs. Ikard told me quietly. I liked Senator Brooks and Walter Cronkite. Ted Kappel was often in DC and would frequently attend parties at their Shepherdstown farm too, but he was not like Mr. Cronkite.

In November 1976, Jimmy Carter was elected the new president of United States, beating out Gerald Ford. I guess people were tired of the sneaky and unethical situation that happened in the Nixon administration. Jimmy Carter's young, clean looks and fresh ideas were a breath of fresh air. People were excited again, and hopeful, just like when Americans elected President Kennedy twenty years prior.

I passed my first graduate classes that semester. Somehow, many Asian students stuck closely to one another. Every afternoon around 2:00pm, the international students from China, Korea, Philippines, Indonesia, Thailand, and Japan would hang out at the Marvin Center. We just had a lot in common: our lifestyles, family lives, and common purpose for making a better way in America.

My friends Tsuchiyama and Harry, a Taiwanese student, and I were thinking about starting an organization. GWU accepted our request, and we established the Asian Student Association. Harry Wu was the first president of this group. We got our own room at Thompson Hall. Tsuchiyama and I discussed that

Japanese students should not hold all of the organization's leadership positions. We were already known for invading and conquering other countries in Asia. So, we were careful to select a variety of members and temper our Japanese pride when socializing with other club members.

At Christmas time, we had our first members-only meeting and held a big party, over 100 attended from more than fifteen different countries. I realized how close we had all gotten since first starting our classes. Everyone brought something to the club dynamic. For example, the students from the Philippines, India, and Thailand were great at organizing parties. It was my first real college party.

Before I knew it, New Year's Day came around again, but it was nothing special. In January, though, I saw the new president walk from the Capitol building to the White House for his inauguration. Our new president and first lady and their little girl Amy were holding hands with each other and waving the crowds lined up behind the safety lines. I felt like a new phase in America had begun.

Kalorama Square

"Massy, can you go to Dulles airport to pick up Mr. Greene tomorrow morning?" Mrs. Ikard asked me one day in March. I agreed quickly. "Yes, I'd be happy to. I like Mr. Green." I parked my station wagon at the arrival deck around 10:00am, and then I quickly checked the status of Mr. Green's flight from Los Angeles. I found out the flight just arrived on time. I went back to the car and waited by the door. Ten minutes later, I saw Mr. Green walk outside. He was wearing a white cowboy hat and a modern suit. I put my hand to Mr. Green, and he nodded to me and started moving towards where the car was parked. I met him halfway, intending to carry his luggage but was swiftly intercepted by the airport police. "Hey! What are you doing?!" one of the policemen held my arm firmly, keeping me away from Mr. Green. Then, the officer's tone shifted completely, suddenly sickeningly sweet, "Mr. Greene, are you okay, sir?" "I'm okay, this is my friend," Mr. Green told him, amused. The airport police looked embarrassed and left quickly. I was glad Mr. Green called me "my friend" not just "he's my ride." We got into the car, and I was eager to leave the situation behind. Mr. Green, trying to ease the tension, said, "let's hit the road, Massy!" *I like him!* "Mr. Green, you look good and happy this morning," I complimented him. "Yeah, Massy, Nancy stayed in Los Angeles this time," he said, winking at me. Nancy was his wife, and I thought she was such a nice woman. Clearly, Mr. Green was ready for some time away. "I'm going to the White House tomorrow and to a couple of parties later on in the week," he continued to tell me. "I'm going to have fun while I'm here!" He stayed at Kalorama Square for five days.

The Ikard's held a formal black tie party two days after I picked Mr. Green up. Mr. Green wore a black western-style tuxedo and looked sharp. I did not know whether there was a main guest or not since there were politicians and high-profile movie stars everywhere I looked.

"Massy, can I hide a lady in your room?" Mr. Green had taken me aside when the party was almost over. "No problem, Mr. Green," I told him. "Okay, I'll bring her, but if somebody asks you about her, you don't know anything, okay?" he asked. A few minutes later, a very attractive blonde-haired woman in her early forties followed him into my room. He left and returned to the party. I left the room but hung nearby, close to the garage entrance. A few minutes later, one gentleman came down to the garage door entrance and asked me, "did you see a pretty woman come down here?" "I'm sorry, I don't know sir," I answered, trying to sound innocent. I recognized this person. He was the Secretary of Energy James Schlesinger. He was well-known at the time due his role in trying to manage the energy crisis. He was tall and strong-looking man. He looked around for a few minutes but eventually gave up and left. Then Mr. Green came back downstairs and asked me, "Massy, did that guy come down here looking for her?" "Yes, he came, but I told him I hadn't seen her." "Good, he's pushed her to go out with him many times but she's not interested," Mr. Green explained. "Anyway, I'm gonna go out with her myself…I may not come back tonight," he smiled casually and winked at me. I didn't know what to think, so I tried to put it out of my mind and enjoy the rest of the evening.

Since I moved to Kalorama Square, the time had gone by so quickly. During the week, I went to school and helped with maintenance for their house. I took care of their small garden which had three pine trees, a Japanese maple, and a variety of flowering plants. Since their property was the largest, being on the end of the row, it also had the most green space and I tried to make sure it was well taken care of. I helped out with their parties of course, usually once every other week, and began to do my own catering for extra income, just about once a week. I would still go to Sushi Ko or another restaurant myself. Once in a while, I would go to dinner with my Japanese friends, but they were rich and would usually want to go to expensive places that I could not afford. I was doing okay at the Ikard's house and studying at GWU, but I was so busy. By the third semester at GW, my grades were just barely at the passing mark, but I wanted to continue with my busy schedule.

As I went about my life with work and school and friends, I also developed a few female friendships. My first female friend was a Korean girl named Young Hui. She was sitting beside me when I took the TOEFL (Test of English as a Foreign Language) at Howard University for admittance into Georgetown University back in 1975. She was so cute and worked as a hair stylist in Leesburg, VA. Sometimes, I would stop by her workplace to see her when I'd go back and tend to the Shepherdstown farm. We were just friends. Sometimes, we would go eat at the Pizza Hut in Leesburg when she got off work. At that time, my pockets were light and I couldn't afford to take someone else to a fancy place. Pizza Hut was cheap but was also a nice romantic place for young people in 1975 or 1976. A year after we started getting to know one another, she had to move to Huntington Beach in California. We did exchange mail for a while, but I was busy in Washington and she was busy with her new place in California. The connection slowly disappeared.

I met a couple other women during my years at Georgetown and GWU. Like my friend group, many of the women were international: Japanese, Korean, Vietnamese, Filipino, and Italian. Many of the Japanese girls were pretty sociable with the American guys, so I was not really interested in dating them. All of the Japanese girls I met were shy and not very outgoing. I did date a few Vietnamese women. There seemed to be a good many Vietnamese people living in Washington at that time. The Vietnam war ended two year earlier, in 1975, and I imagined that had an impact on the large population living in DC. There are so many wealthy Vietnamese families living here and many of their young adults attended Georgetown, GWU, and American University. Many of the Vietnamese college students got together once a month to socialize and dance at one of Georgetown's nightclubs. I was invited there once a while by my friend. On the stage, they featured singers who sang Vietnamese songs, which were quite similar to Japanese songs.

Many Vietnamese people I knew missed their country. Some who were higher ranking military officials, those in government positions, or wealthy businesspeople gathered all their family and belongings and fled their places fearing for their safety. So I guessed that they wanted to get together just once a month in memory of their country and the lives they left behind there. One of my Vietnamese friends, Thui, introduced me to a petite Japanese girl named Kimi who attended Catholic University. She was only eighteen years old and stood at barely five feet high. With her short boyish hairstyle and small frame, she looked like she was only fifteen or sixteen years old. I became close to Kimi quickly. Because she was so young, I was kind of worried about her since her dormitory near Rhode Island Ave had a lot of recent crimes. I would walk her to her dormitory once in a while and take her out to a restaurant or to see a movie. One night, we went to go see *A Star is Born*, featuring Barbara Streisand. It was my first movie theater in Washington, DC, and my second movie in the States.

But, late that May, I had to return to Martha's Vineyard with the Ikard's for a third summer. "I'm in Boston visiting my friend. Is it possible for us to meet up?" Kimi had called me on the telephone at Martha's Vineyard. "Yeah, I may be able see you," I told her, "but I have to talk with Mrs. Ikard first to make sure I can take some time away." I was not sure that I should talk to Mrs. Ikard to get permission for to go to Boston especially since I was going to meet up with a girl. I didn't know what she would think, but I worked up the courage to talk to her. "Mrs. Ikard, may I take a few days off to go to Boston and see a friend who is there visiting?" "Sure, no problem." Mrs. Ikard smiled. "Are you meeting with a girl?" she asked, as if she could sense the reason for my hesitation in asking. "Yes, a Japanese girl," I admitted. "Of course you can go to Boston, Massy, and you can bring her here to Martha's Vineyard if you like. She might enjoy it here," Mrs. Ikard went on. I felt so happy with her response. So I went to Boston in July.

Boston was a beautiful and historic city. It had a nice downtown and Chinatown area. Across the Charles River, Cambridge was scenic too. There were many ivy league colleges like Harvard and MIT. Their campuses were impressive and the college town was lined with cozy shops and eateries. We stayed in Boston two days before I brought Kimi back to the island, where she stayed with me for three days. We went to everywhere in Martha's Vineyard. It was the first time I had actually taken a break from work and actually enjoyed myself. Kimi was a good cook, too, and great at baking cookies. I could tell Mr. and Mrs. Ikard liked having Kimi there, too. I had grown to like spending the summers in Martha's Vineyard and this one was particularly memorable.

That fall, in October 1977, Mr. and Mrs. Ikard had another one of their famous parties at Kalorama Square. They were supporting the formation of the American Negro College Fund. The ambassador of the United Nations, Andrew Young, came with a lot of lovely Black women. More than 100 people came. Mr. Young was a handsome man, just like movie star. Wherever he moved about the room, all the young ladies followed him.

My academic standing was okay, but I was more involved in school activities and gathering with friends. Every week it felt like my schedule was packed. Some of my friends got their degrees and prepared to go back to Japan. Tokken, Kaneko, and Kobayashi were leaving after the end of the semester. More Japanese students came to GW and joined the Asian Student Association, but I wasn't as close with them as the friends I entered GW with. Kimi also moved to another state. She was accepted to the University of Wisconsin, Green Bay as a psychology major.

Green Card

It was a pretty quiet year in 1978. Many of my friends left Washington. But my routine was the same as before: I stayed with the Ikard's and cleaned their home, took classes at GW, and went to Sushi Ko a few times a week. Occasionally, I'd go to a Korean piano bar called East Paradise. Once every few weeks, I'd get a catering job. Classes at GW were getting harder, but I was managing it okay.

"Massy, what are you going to do after school?" Carmen, the Ikard's Peruvian maid, asked me one day in springtime. She was short with a warm smile. She was friendly to me and the other staff. Sometimes she would talk about her husband who drank too much or would tell be about her family and parents in Peru. "I'm not sure, but I definitely don't want to go back to Japan," I told her. "Will you get a job here? What about making your own business?" "It depends," I replied. "I still only have a student visa." "What? You don't have a green card? Mr. Ikard didn't give you one?" She looked surprised. "No, not yet." I paused. "Mr. Ikard hasn't said anything to me about it." "I thought you would have already had a green card because you've worked here such a long time," she said before she saw my face fall. "I'm sure Mr. Ikard will give you one very soon," she added. "I don't know. He hasn't said anything to me about it in a long time," I said, my frustration coming through. "Massy, if you're interested, I can introduce you to a place where you might be able to get legal help without having to pay anything," Carmen told me. I could tell she was trying to help.

She introduced me to some people from the immigration legal services at Catholic Charities. I called them and made an appointment. I did not tell Mr. Ikard anything about it. The place was in downtown Washington on the corner of K Street and 14th Street. It looked look like an old government building. "You've been in the US since 1974? And you've been working for Mr. Ikard?" Mrs. Johnson asked once I was seated in a small room. Mrs. Johnson was a woman in her fifties with brown hair and a Spanish accent. Her gentle demeanor made me feel comfortable right away. "Yes," I told her. "And you go to GWU?" she asked. "Yes," I said again. "I have a student visa." "Massy, you are lucky. Mr. Ikard is very special. His name is in this green book," she said, patting a green-fabric covered book with her palm. "This green book is Washington DC's high society information book. Anyone listed here should have no problem requesting a green card for their workers. You may get your green card soon without any trouble," she went on confidently. My face lit up. *It couldn't be that easy, could it?* "Oh my god! Thank you, Mrs. Johnson! How much do I owe you this starting this paperwork process?" I asked her. "No, no," she said, waving her arms in front of her. "You don't owe anything; this organization is a non-profit for people like you who need legal help." I felt like I had won the lottery.

Two or three days later, I heard Mr. Ikard calling downstairs to me when he came back from his office. "Massy, do you know Mrs. Johnson?" "Yes, Carmen introduced her place to me," I told him plainly. I felt my body stiffen up, hoping he would not be mad I had gone without telling him. But, I took a deep breath and reassured myself that I had done the right thing. He knew from the beginning I needed a green card to stay and work for him and had not followed through with his offer. "The Catholic Charities is a great organization. I signed all your documents this afternoon. You will get your green card soon, and I'm sorry I forgot to submit your visa for permanent status," Mr. Ikard said. I wondered how he could forget my status for such a long time. *Did he truly forget or did he think I would leave his service as soon as I got my card? I had been with the Ikard's for many years working hard for little money or status. So why would he delay helping me secure a green card?* I didn't know. But what was the use in saying anything now? I would have my green card soon. So I just smiled and told him evenly, "Sorry Mr. Ikard that I didn't mention that I had gone there sooner." "No problem. It's all good." He walked back upstairs and left me on the lower level at the bottom of the staircase.

That September 1978, I got my green card. I felt the anxiety and stress about my status just melt away. *Now I have a real chance,* I thought. It was something I had wanted so badly since the first time I set foot in America. I invited Mrs. Johnson to have dinner with me at the Japanese restaurant Mikado on Wisconsin Avenue to celebrate and thank her for her help. Mikado was a small restaurant but was always very busy.

They kept real Japanese foods in stock just like restaurants in Japan. It was one of the most authentic places in DC and I was glad to have someone who knew what this meant for me be there with me to enjoy a tasty meal and relax. Mrs. Johnson loved the food, which made me feel even better.

There were only three Japanese restaurants in Washington: Mikado, Tokyo Sukiyaki, and Sushi Ko. Sushi Ko was the restaurant I most often went to, mostly because it had a sushi bar that was true to Japanese style. Mikado was more high quality, and more expensive, plus it had a larger variety of Japanese dishes. The owner was a retired Japanese Embassy chief chef. Tokyo Sukiyaki was the oldest Japanese restaurant in the city, but around that time all their good chefs had left and it was being run by an old Korean woman. After a while, I just stopped going.

✦✦✦

After getting my green card, I found that I could focus on school a little more. I thought that by May 1979, I would be able to graduate with my Master's degree. My goal was challenging because I still needed to finish my final thesis. It was a complex paper and even though I could focus more then, I knew finishing by my goal date would be difficult.

In the Spring of 1979, I was well on my way to meeting my graduation goal. Then, a strongly-worded letter arrived in the mail from my brother: *I understand that you will get your Master's degree soon. Please think about coming back to Japan. Why don't you make Mom happy? I don't mind being the one to stay here with Mom for a long time, but Mom needs you, too. Plus, you might get a much better job with a higher degree. The employment system has changed so much in the past few years, too. There's no more lifetime employment—it is not like before when you were here. There are so many foreign companies looking for Japanese people with a higher educational background and an English language proficiency. Please consider it.*

I knew my brother had married the year before, and it was a traditional Japanese custom that the oldest son, me, must take care of my parents as well as the growing Hirai family to keep our family name and legacy preserved forever. But I left Japan over five years ago and left that way of thinking behind, too. I'm sure my brother loves our Mom, but my brother may think that he is now independent since he is beginning his own family. *Maybe I am too stubborn and selfish.* Even though I never doubted leaving, I always felt so sorry to my mother and what my leaving meant for her. I called to my brother a week after receiving his letter, once I had some time to collect my thoughts and process what he was asking of me. "Yo chan, my brother," I began. "I understand one hundred percent why you said what you did and your reasons for asking me to come back. I'm sorry. I think I need to stay here and continue to establish my life in America," I told him, trying to sound confident in what I was saying. He paused for a brief moment, caught off guard by what I was saying. "No!" He was angry. "You should think more about our family!" he said sternly, before adding "and you did not do anything for your future yet! Just think about this decision more deeply. You have a chance at a good life here too-not everything is better in America. Japan still offers so much, and you don't even realize it!" As he kept talking, his voice had gotten louder and louder. "Yo chan, please," I said, trying to calm him (and myself). I have to continue what I started here. I may be wrong or I may be right, but I just got my green card. I can't give up now because I've been working so hard for this chance. Please try and see things from my perspective too," I pleaded. It was no use. "Aniki, older brother, you are too selfish. You should think one more time." We were clearly at an impasse and left the call there.

His words stuck with me long after the call ended. I wondered, *am I a bad person and son?* I had no idea it was going to be such a problem for my family when I decided to make my own way and take a chance to build my own future. My brother is a very thoughtful person, but very traditional and narrow-minded. Many Japanese men are the same as my brother when it comes to keeping aligned with long-standing traditions and not going against the cultural grain. I know that my mother missed me a lot and worried about my future, and therefore my brother worried too. They felt I had enough time to go off independently on my own in the US and make my own way. They figured that with a higher education degree from an American school that I would come back better off than when I had left. I understood their position exactly. *Maybe they were right.* My future in the US was not clear and it had taken me much longer than I antici-pated to get my green card and finish school. I knew I didn't have much to show for all the time I spent here, but I could still imagine a better and more fulfilling life. I knew I didn't want to go back to Japan.

A couple weeks later, I worked up the nerve to share what was in my heart. "I'm sorry, Yo chan," I told him truthfully. "I don't mean to hurt you or mom. But I've thought deeply about this and made my decision. I'm going to stay here." I said the words carefully but clearly. My brother was so angry with me that he hung up the phone.

It took me several weeks before I could get my brother's stinging words off my mind. I went to Korean night club in the city that had live music. I sat in the back hall, listened to Japanese songs, and drank scotch my myself and let the tears flow. I thought about my mother and chided myself for focusing so much on myself and my life. I almost felt angry with myself for not being able to take the good advice from people who loved me and for pushing forward with my goals no matter the cost. It was almost the same feeling I had when I left Japan five years ago on the airplane between Tokyo and Hawaii. Maybe it was listening to Japanese songs that made me nostalgic. I had been here before, always by myself and towards the back side of the club. Mrs. Lee, the owner of the night club, recognized me and waved. She always made polite small talk with me about how my school was going or how my family was doing back in Japan. I was grateful that night to see a kind face in the crowd. It lifted my spirits. I stayed another few hours until the scotch wore off and then drove back home. Driving my Ford Gran Torino station wagon with the driver's side window open and the wind blowing on my face helped me clear my mind. I passed the Pentagon on my left side, passed the stone Memorial Bridge, and took Rock Creek Park Drive. From there, I passed under the Kennedy Center ,drove another five minutes, and went up Massachusetts Avenue. In front of me I saw the Washington Mosque, and on my right side, on the corner, was the Canadian

Embassy. *Kalorama Square is only 3 more blocks.* I now had the roads memorized. Between the music and the cool drive, I began to feel much better.

"Massy, can you clean our second floor today?" Mrs. Ikard asked me the next morning. "Yes, ma'am. Is something special happening tonight?" I asked her. "We invited some guests to come over. I think you'll recognize them," she responded, giggling a little. Later that day when I was cleaning out my car in the garage (the Kalorama Square garage was all underground), a sleek, full-sized, black Mercedes sedan came to a stop in front of me. "Is the Ikard residence is here?" came a beautiful voice from the window as it was being rolled down. I was taken back by who poked her head out of the window. I looked at her. It was none other than Elizabeth Taylor. "Yes, you're right here," I said, almost in disbelief. When I looked over at the driver's side, I saw strong-looking, distinguished man. I realized he was the new Senator from Virginia. John Warner. They held each other's hands each other and whispered to each other all night. I had seen Elizabeth Taylor at the Ikard residence before for some of their parties but never so closely. She was even more dazzling close up and had a voice like tinkling bells. I was surprised she had forgotten which house it was but also figured she must have been to so many nice residences all over the country that it would be easy to get lost.

That whole evening felt like Hollywood had come to DC. Guests included Mr. and Mrs. Lorne Green, Mr. Danny Kaye, and of course, Elizabeth Taylor and Senator John Warner. Mr. and Mrs. Greene were staying at the Washington Hilton hotel, two blocks away from Kalorama Square. And I saw Danny Kaye first time. He was skinny and looked so much older than he had when starring in the movie *White Christmas*. The party was lively and they spent most of the evening in the dining room. Whenever I went to go refill glasses or bring out more dishes, Mr. Green was animatedly telling stories while the others were just listening. Senator Warner and Elizabeth Taylor gazed at each other and had their hands entwined until Warner was ready to light a cigar. He enjoyed his smoke and then they retired to the living room upstairs where they listened to live piano music. The piano man was kind of smiling and enjoyed playing his tunes, happy to have an audience at last. Until someone went upstairs, the piano man was just easy background music playing to an empty room. Danny Kaye was frail looking, but when he danced, he seemed years younger. His face gained color, and he let his body move freely to the rhythm. The Ikard's had the evening catered by Dave's Catering, which was a local, Black-owned business. One of the servers was a seventy-two year old woman, who had recently been featured in the Style section of the Washington Post for serving three US presidents. Mr. and Mrs. Ikard would usually reserve Dave's Catering for special events. The end of May, the Ikard's had once again made their yearly trip up north to Martha's Vineyard. Something felt different about this summer of 1979. I felt as though it might be my last trip there for a while. "Massy, can you take me to Martha's Vineyard?" Mr. Ikard asked me. "Sure, no problem. Will Mrs. Ikard be riding with us too?" I asked him. "No, she flew to Boston to meet up with some friends first," he replied. "It'll just be the two of us." I was a little nervous. It was the first time I had driven so far with just Mr. Ikard. When we left Kalorama Square, I heard the loud click of Mr. Ikard's seat belt, which was strange to me because he never wore a seat belt. At that time, there is no seatbelt mandate and it was not commonplace for people to wear them unless they had a specific reason to need one. I was worried Mr. Ikard didn't trust my driving or thought I might speed. I knew I'd need to pay extra attention to the road for this trip and was a bit disappointed I would not have a relaxing drive.

But, I was wrong. It was actually a pleasant drive with Mr. Ikard and went much faster than expected because we had many nice conversations along the way. I was able to share with him how much I enjoyed being in the US and told him about the dilemma I was having regarding my plan for future and my family's desire for me to go back to Japan. It was the real talk we had in a long while, and I thought maybe it would the last time we'd be able to have an uninterrupted conversation. "Mr. Ikard, how you know so many famous people?" I asked. He thought for a second before admitting, "I don't know many, but Mrs. Ikard knows a lot." He continued, "You know, Mrs. Ikard used to be a journalist, which is how she knows so many people," he said. "By the way, Massy, what will you do next? I mean, now that you have your green card," Mr. Ikard wondered out loud. "I really just don't know yet, Mr. Ikard" I answered him. I wished I knew.

Honestly, all I could think about was finishing my thesis and graduating with my Master's degree. Then, I figured I would probably go into the food business. I had done well with catering and had always had so many compliments when I would cook for the Ikard's and their guests. I never really thought about job hunting in the US, for I don't want to get the same situation I had in Japan, working for someone else year after year without any outside life or real impact on the company. The desire to work for myself and create my way of life was one of the biggest reasons I had come here. Maki, one of my Japanese friends, told me that her fiancé, Fumio, would also be graduating that year with a Master's degree this year, and that he was able to line up a job at the World Bank. Maybe I could get a job at the World Bank, too? It was hard to say.

Back in the station wagon, Mr. Ikard went on. He told me, "Massy, I don't want to hold you back, so if you decide to go on and do something else, go! We understand and want you to go for your dreams." That felt so good to hear after working tirelessly for them the past five years. I smiled a genuine smile, and replied, "I would very much like to stay with you and Mrs. Ikard a little longer. I'll be at GWU at least until the end of the school year." He nodded, "Whatever you choose to do, we will support you. You have worked hard and been very good for us." It was the acknowledgement I had waiting so long for and hoped to hear.

As the summer went on, I became more certain that this would be my last summer with the Ikard's at Martha's Vineyard. Whenever I had free time in the afternoons, I would take the path down to the state beach, near Oak Bluffs where Jaws was filmed, and lay down on the bare sand and think about my options for the future or doze off. I felt so comfortable, looking out at the horizon and the lapping waves near the shoreline. I thought about how much different I was than the typical Japanese man who would be mid-career by now. I would be 32 years old soon and had no idea where I would be or what I would be doing a year from then.

✦ ✦ ✦

MEET JUN

My last semester at GWU began in September 1979. Although
I felt I were at a crossroads, my schedule was still the same as
it had been before: working at Ikard's, going to school, taking
catering jobs once in a while for extra cash, and going to restaurants or night clubs occasionally. One evening that month,
my friend Maki and I went to Shokudoen, a Korean night club
in Crystal City, VA. Miss Cho, a Korean singer, was singing there
live. I had been there before but thought Maki might enjoy
the music, too. Once we were seated and enjoying a drink,
Maki nudged me. "Massy, she is singing a Japanese song!" she
exclaimed. "Yeah, she does occasionally. If I'm here, she sings
more Japanese songs," I told her, smiling. The song ended and I
heard a loud voice come over the microphone. "The next song
is for Massy," Miss Cho announced, looking right at me. My
face went red and I looked up at her. "Massy, does she know
you?" Maki whispered to me. "I have not talked to her before,"
I replied, thinking hard. "Maybe the owner Mrs. Lee told her
about me?" Maki and I had been good friends for a few years
at GW; she had transferred from England after my first year of
classes. Maki's fiancé, Fumio, went to Cornell University, so she
did not see him often. Sometimes we would get together to have
dinner or go watch music when he was busy with school.

I went again the following night, this time by myself. Feeling
bold, I asked the waitress, "please ask Miss Cho to come to
my table and enjoy a drink with me." Soon enough, Miss Cho

approached my table and smiled down at me. "Can I have a seat here?" she asked. She had long, thick, curly hair and heavy makeup for the stage. "Thank you for coming. Would you like a drink?" "Just an orange juice please. I can't drink alcohol," she explained. I ordered her the orange juice and then made conversation. "Thank you for always singing Japanese songs," I told her. "No problem," she said. "I noticed you come here quite often, and Mrs. Lee shared that you are a special customer." She didn't know much English, but we still had a nice talk, switching from English to Japanese. She had only been in the US for six months, but mostly stayed with Korean populations in LA and Washington, DC. There are not many Japanese customers at the restaurant, I noticed, and most people who came were Korean.

We talked about our families and home countries and our jobs. I found out she came to the US on an entertainment visa and performed in many cities. Towards the end of the night, I asked her, "Would you like to go to a Japanese restaurant when you have off day?" "Okay, thank you. I have off tomorrow," she replied. "I'll take you tomorrow then," I offered.

Around 6:00pm the next day, I went to a new townhouse in Crystal City near the Pentagon and pressed the doorbell. It looked like she had been waiting for me, for the door opened quickly. Her lovely face smiled at me, and then I realized an older lady behind her was smiling at me too. I wasn't expecting to see anyone but Miss Cho. "Thank you for inviting me to dinner, too," the older lady asserted. I tried not to let my surprise show on my face. "Okay, let's go," I said to them both. Miss Cho introduced me to the woman before we left. "This is Kay," she told me. "I am staying her house, and we are very good friends, too." Maybe she invited her friend to make sure she was safe? It was hard to say.

Shokudoen, the Korean night club, had a contract with Kay to home their entertainers who were staying in Washington, DC.

Miss Cho had been there a few months already and was halfway through her stay. Then she would move on to another city. We went to Mikado. Even though it was a weeknight, the restaurant was busy, so while we waited for a table we went and stood outside the restaurant. That wasn't unusual, for Mikado was very small and cozy, with only about ten tables. We were seated and didn't have to wait too long to get our food. Miss Cho and Kay were enjoying their meals. Kay was about 40 years old and was very friendly. She owned a hair salon near her home. "Massy, why did you come to the US?" she asked me politely. "Well, I was looking for a new life, and a challenge," I replied. She looked intently at my face and seemed to be thinking. I understood that many Koreans immigrated to the US because of their political situation between North and South Korea. Many of them had painful war experiences, and they were simply searching for peace. Many Japanese immigrants came to US over a hundred years ago, for similar reasons. I wondered if that's what brought Kay here, but I didn't want to bring up a subject that was tender, so I changed the subject.

We went to Blues Alley in Georgetown after Mikado. "Massy, Miss Cho was a jazz singer in Korea," Kay leaned close and told me. We had been seated at a table right in front of the stage. This Jazz club was small, and the stage and customers were so close to one another. People were smoking, and the room looked hazy. "This is very good place. I feel like we are in New Orleans," Miss Cho said happily. It seemed like she was enjoying herself. I thought it was rather special, too. After a lively evening, I dropped them at Kay's townhouse. "Massy, please come to visit us any time," Kay told me.

Nearly a month passed. "Massy, what is going on? You haven't gone out in the evening for a long time," Mrs. Ikard remarked. It was almost the end of October in 1979. "Mrs. Ikard, I am little behind on my final thesis," I admitted. "I have to submit them soon if I want to graduate," I told her. "I've never seen you study before, but now you look like a student!" Mrs. Ikard smiled and said. I turned once again to my writing. At the beginning of the month, I had gone to see my academic adviser to make sure I had everything in order to finish school that semester. "Mr. Hirai, you are on the borderline for your degree. How is your final paper going?" Professor Kennedy, my adviser, asked, seeming concerned. I knew my grades weren't the best, and even though I already gave my topic for the thesis to my adviser, I had not submitted my thesis draft to him. "Hopefully, your thesis will be strong," he told me. I couldn't stop now.

During Thanksgiving time, as per the Ikard family tradition, all the children came to Washington. That year, though, things were a little different because Mr. Ikard's sons did not come with their wives. Frank came himself, and Bill came with his girlfriend, Kathy Cronkite, the daughter of Walter Cronkite (Lisa and Bill divorced the previous year). "We have now two Cathy's, but one is C and other is K," Mrs. Ikard laughed. Mrs. Ikard's son Bryan just gotten engaged to a young woman named Cathy Brown. It was kind of a quiet Thanksgiving, which I didn't mind.

The first week of December Professor Kennedy called me and said, "Congratulations, Mr. Hirai. Your graduate studies are complete and you've earned your Master's degree!" "It was very close," he continued. "But you did very good work on your thesis." He congratulated me again and we got off the phone. I was ecstatic. I went upstairs and told Mrs. Ikard that I got my MBA. "Massy we are so proud of you! We will take you to a nice restaurant and celebrate," Mrs. Ikard said. They took me to the one of best French restaurants in the city, Sans Souci. It was second time they had taken me out to a restaurant; they had taken me to a Chinese restaurant in 1974. But, it was the first time I enjoyed an alcoholic beverage in their presence. I had a wonderful time that night with Mr. and Mrs. Ikard. Even though it was a congratulations dinner, I also felt as though they suspected my imminent departure and treated it as a farewell dinner also.

After all, I had my green card now and a Master's degree from an American university, so they must have known that I would be ready to move on and begin the next chapter of my journey. As the Christmas holiday approached, I went to Shokudoen, the Korean night club, again. "What happened? You have not been here in a long time," Miss Cho said when she approached my table during her break. "I'm sorry, but I've been so busy trying to finish school," I admitted to her. "Please come to Kay's house after you leave here?" Miss Cho asked me. Kay's townhouse is near the Pentagon and was only 10 minutes from the DC downtown area. It was built in a nice community complex, like Kalorama Square, and had a cozy garden area, too.

When I arrived at Kay's house later that night, there were several other people already there. "Massy, let me introduce you to Mr. Lee and his friends," Kay told me. "Mr. Lee is a singer, too," she added. He smiled when he heard her mention his name, stood up, and came over to shake my hand. He was a good-looking man about fifty years of age. "How do you do?" he said, making his introductions. As we chatted, he told me about his heritage and that his grandmother was Japanese. He shared, "my grandmother was from the Japanese Emperor's family." I just looked at him for a minute, stunned. "Wow! Is that true?" I wondered in amazement. I heard a long time ago that when the Japanese government took over Korea over a hundred years prior, they sent the youngest sister of Meiji Emperor for marriage to the last male member of the Korean Lee Dynasty. There are so many political marriages arranged for their own benefit in our human history. I felt a bit strange in front of Mr. Lee for the rest of the night. I was sure that if his grandmother was indeed part of this union that she must have had a hard time with the marriage, especially considering the trauma caused by the Japanese invasion of her country. For many Japanese people, some still believe the Emperor is a kind of God, on a much different level from the common people. This power extended through his lineage. There I was, standing only a foot away from his family.

I went to Shokudoen the next day to listen to Mr. Lee's songs. He sang both jazz and American pop styles. I wondered whether any of the political figures in the room knew who Mr. Lee was or not. He was just a civilian in this place and time, but if Korea had still a monarch system, he could be a Prince or Emperor. I listened to his song, thinking that he looked just like Jackie Chan and feeling curious about what his upbringing and personal life were like. I didn't know how the Korean government could cut their royal family for position, benefit, security, or income. First of all, I wondered how Mr. Lee must feel being from a royal family to just being as a civilian. I wanted to ask him so much. Of course, I considered that he may not want to talk about this issue with a person he met just yesterday. The following week, I took Miss Cho to the blues club, Blues Alley, in Georgetown. Famous McCoy Tyner was there. I did not know much about jazz, but I knew McCoy Tyner was a top jazz musician. I loved the atmosphere in the club, how the audience would sit very close together at their tiny tables with the stage performers mere feet away. It almost felt as if they were playing among us and the whole room was filled with the rhythm of the piano. The dim lights and thick, smoky haze added to its unique ambiance. Afterward, we went to the French cafe La Ruche beside Georgetown's canal on 31st Street. At the cafe, we sat close together. Miss Cho pulled something out of her pocket. Here, I made this for you; you might need it soon," she said. Inside a fancy bag was a pair of hand-knit gloves. Miss Cho surprised me. I didn't know any entertainers in Japan, but she definitely was not what I expected, a famous singer who knitted gloves and brought her friend along for first dates. I soon realized that Miss Cho was a family-oriented person. I soon began to visit her at Miss Kay's house at least once a week or more.

Whenever I went to Kay's, she always prepared homestyle Korean dishes. It really was my first time enjoying Korean foods with Korean people. In Japan, it was impossible to see Korean and Japanese people sitting and enjoying a meal together. Actually, it was quite refreshing to realize that not all Korean people hated Japanese people. As we spoke about our countries, I realized that there were more similarities between Korea and Japan than I previously thought. Even our languages were similar in that the subject and object preceded the verb in sentences. Our food customs were similar too, for each person used small plates and most dishes came with short-grain sticky rice. Finally, our family beliefs were similar in each culture too, especially when it came to men's value for carrying on the family name and legacy.

1980 came before I knew it. Ever since I came to the United States, time seemed to have passed much more quickly than my life before in Japan. "Massy, I have little sad news today," Kay told me when I visited her house shortly after the new year arrived. "Oh, no. What happened?" "Miss Cho may go to New York soon when her contract is up. She asked her manager whether she could stay here in DC, but they need her to move on soon," Kay told me, shaking her head sadly. "Is there anything we can do to help her?" I asked. "I don't think so. It sounds like a difficult situation," she replied.

Two or three days later, Kay called me and asked me if I could come to her house. She sat me down on the couch in her living room and looked at me intently for a minute. She licked her lips and then spoke. "Massy, a few days ago you asked whether you could help Miss Cho." "Of course, " I said curiously. "I'd be happy to help her if I could." "Well, I think there might be a way," she told me tentatively. "Okay, so… if you don't feel comfortable, please tell me. You have a green card, so if you two were to get engaged, she could get an engagement visa and stay in the US legally for at least a year. If that were the case, she would have more flexibility on the singing tour rather than be moved from city to city by her manager. She would be able to pick where she wants to go…" Kay explained, trailing off. "Well, that's easy," I said, smiling. "Of course I can do that." "Are you sure? You don't have to answer now," she said quickly. "Yes, I'm sure. It's really no problem," I reassured her. "Oh, this is wonderful. She will be very happy tonight when I tell her the good news!" Kay's face lit up, and I knew I was doing the right thing. As soon as I got back to the Ikard's, I got a phone call from Miss Cho. "Thank you so much!!" I could tell she was elated. "How can I return the favor?" she asked me. "No problem, this is nothing," I said, laughing. "I'm just happy to help."

A couple days later, Miss Cho and I went to a Korean lawyer's office, Kay's contact, to sign and notarize the paperwork for the engagement visa. I did not think deeply when I signed the engagement paperwork because I figured this was just an engagement, not a marriage, and it didn't impact my own legal paperwork any. Later that evening, once the paperwork was complete, Kay pulled me aside. "Massy, thank you for helping Miss Cho. She wants to pay to you, but she said you don't want any money?" she asked curiously. I shook my head side to side. "No," I told her firmly. "These days, documents like this can cost up to $10,000 for a fake marriage and $3,000 for a fake engagement on the black market," she continued. I wasn't interested in the money. I liked Miss Cho and wanted her to have the option to stay and sing where she wanted to be.

The next month, in February, Mrs. Ikard had news. "Massy, Mr. Ikard and I are going to Denmark next week for 5 days," she announced after dinner one evening. "Can you go to our house in Martha's Vineyard and take some paintings and home items while we are gone?" she asked. "Yes, Mrs. Ikard. I'd be happy to." I had never been to Martha's Vineyard in the wintertime and was excited to see what the off-season was like there.

The next day, the phone rang. It was Miss Cho, inviting me to a nice dinner on Valentine's Day. "I'm so sorry," I told her, declining the offer, "but I have to go Martha's Vineyard and pack up some things for the Ikard's." "Martha's Vineyard? Where's that?" she asked. "It's an island in Massachusetts." "An island? So you have to get there by boat? Wow!" she exclaimed. "Yeah, they have a second home there. It's very beautiful, and I've never been there in winter before." I paused. I wanted to ask her to go with me and experience it together, but I thought I'd better have a conversation with the Ikard's first. So we hung up, and I went upstairs to find Mrs. Ikard.

I got right to the point. "Mrs. Ikard, is it okay if I take a friend when I go to Martha's Vineyard?" I asked. She smiled warmly and said, "sure, of course. You just drive safely there." I think she knew Miss Cho was the person I planned to invite. I thanked her and called back Miss Cho. I knew she'd be pleased with my news. I was right "Wow! That is wonderful! Thank you, Massy. Can Kay go with us, too?" "Okay," I agreed. I liked Kay but had hoped to spend time with Miss Cho alone. We left Washington a few days later. The drive went so much faster than before when I was alone. We kept a steady stream of conversation the whole way, and Miss Cho sang some of her songs, too. Kay knew so many people. She asked me to stop in New York City because one of her friends, a Korean singer named Ha Nang Gou, was working at a night club called Flushing. "Kay, I know Mr. Ha too! I went to East Paradise many times," I told her. Mr. Ha was singing at another Korean night club in Falls Church, Virginia, that I would go to sometimes with my friend Maki. They had karaoke too. Mr. Ha played piano and sang Japanese songs, too. I took Mr. Ha to Mr. Ikard's farm in Shepherdstown before, too. It was so funny that Kay and I both knew him.

So we stopped by the Korean night club in New York. It was insanely crowded, but Mr. Ha found our table quickly during his break. "Hi! Kay and Massy, we all know each other? And Miss Cho, too! What a small world," he exclaimed, clapping me on the back. "Massy, Miss Cho is a great girl," he pulled me aside and whispered a bit later when she got up to go use the restroom. After catching up a bit, he had to get back to performing and we got back on the road. We arrived at the ferry port at Woods Hole, Massachusetts around 4:00am. Tired from the long drive, I put my seat back and tried to rest my eyes until it was time for the first ferry departure at 6:30am.

6:30am came quickly, and Kay and Miss Cho were awake. "I feel good! This is my first experience taking a ferry boat," Miss Cho told me, clearly excited. Kay seemed to share her enthusiasm. We found three deck chairs on the top floor of the boat and watched the seagulls flying close to us looking for food. We watched the sunrise and before we knew it, the sky turned from dark blue, to a light purple, and soon enough was sky blue. White puffy clouds floated by and the sun's heat soon warmed us. It was going to be a beautiful day. We arrived to the Ikard's house on N. Water St in Edgartown around 9:00am. We unloaded our things quickly before falling asleep.

Later that afternoon, I showed Kay and Miss Cho around the island: Jaws bridge, Menemsha, Gay Head, Vineyard Haven, and finally downtown Edgartown. We were browsing in a gift shop window in Edgartown when somebody called from behind me. "Massy, hi!" It was Senator Brooks. "How are you?" he asked, shaking my hand vigorously. "Senator, how are you? I haven't seen you in a long time. You look well, " I replied happily. It had been at least two or three years since I had seen him. He had come to visit the Ikard's farm in Shepherdstown many times with Barbara Walters but had not come around nearly as often once they parted ways. "I'm fine, just fine! Still keeping busy," he said, grinning, before introducing us to the pretty young woman standing beside him. "This is my friend Silvia, from Saudi Arabia." "Glad to meet you," I told her. Likewise, I introduced him to Miss Cho and Kay. "Are the Ikard's here? I don't see them around much in the winter," the Senator mused. "No they are in Europe but asked me to come and collect some housing things," I explained. He nodded. I didn't ask him what he was doing here in wintertime, assuming that because it was his home state that he had a second home here like the Ikard's did. We chatted for a few minutes longer before saying our good byes and continuing to window shop. "He seems nice," Kay commented when they were far enough away not to hear us anymore. "Yeah, he's a good man and the first Black senator in America," I told her, nodding. As the Senator and Silvia walked down the block, I noticed they were holding hands and gazing at each other. They looked at peace with one another, and I felt happy for him.

I hadn't realized before this trip that so many Native Americans still lived here, too. I got to talking one day with an old woman who owned a small seafood restaurant in Menemsha that had been in her family for five generations. She explained that many of the Native Americans still living here were now fisherman. I remembered the unique housing styles near Menemsha Bay with small porches on their rooftops where the old fishermen would go to watch whales and incoming schools of fish. When I first came to Martha's Vineyard, it was the New England-style homes, locally-owned stores, and beautiful landscaping that drew me to it. But my appreciation for the place had grown deeper over the years as I explored more of the island and learned about its rich history, culture, and Native People who inhabited it long before it was filled with large vacation homes.

When we got back, I brought Kay and Miss Cho over to Kalorama Square because they wanted to meet the Ikard's and thank them for allowing them the visit. "Mrs. Ikard, these are my friends Kay and Cho." "How do you do?" Mrs. Ikard said.

"Thank you very much for letting us visit your house in Martha's Vineyard. We had a wonderful trip," Kay said warmly. "I'm glad you were able to join Massy. It's lovely up there in the winter," she said beaming, clearly glad they wanted to come thank her for the stay.

I fell back easily into my routine: help Mr. and Mrs. Ikard at home, take on occasional catering jobs, have meals sometimes at Sushi Ko, and spend time at Kay's house. My brother called me in early March. "Aniki (older brother), are you coming home? You can get a job easy, and Mother wants to you come home, too." It was always the same conversation. "Sorry, Yochan," I said, trying to keep my voice light and even. "I've already decided to stay in America. I'm not coming back to Japan." I felt he knew my answer already, so he was not angry this time. We spent a short time making easy conversation before hanging up. *I don't know why I just continued to stay. I'm just too stubborn.* Maybe I was thinking about Miss Cho as a more than just a friend. Our relationship had just started to feel comfortable and I thought perhaps it could be a special relationship. I was 33 years old. Miss Cho was 30 years old. She was still singing at Shokudoen almost every night. We went out once in a while. She liked to go to Georgetown, so we would go to Sushi Ko and a fancy Vietnam restaurant called Germaine's on the 2400 block of Wisconsin Ave. The last time we were there, people said Mick Jagger had visited.

Kay called me early April, sounding worried. "Massy, I know you helped a lot, but you're support for Miss Cho isn't going to last any longer," she told me. "What happened?" "The law has changed," she went on. "My friend told me yesterday that the fiancé visa isn't being recognized anymore." So here we were again, back at square one. I knew if I was really going to help her, that I'd have to apply for a marriage license. My mind briefly wandered, and I could just imagine my mom and brother's reaction. "Massy, are you listening me?" Kay asked sharply. "I heard you, but I need some time to think," I told her and hung up phone. I flopped down on my bed and ran through possibilities for my future. Yes, our relationship had developed more as time passed. I thought about her family in Korea. I don't think that her family would agree to marry her to a Japanese man. Plus, she was the eldest sibling and might have other family responsibilities. But the important factor was her own desire about a future with me—or not. So far, I could see that she liked me. But I didn't want marriage to just be a solution to her legal problem. In order to know, I would have to express my feelings for her and see if she felt the same in return.

The following week, at Sushi Ko, I mustered up the courage to address things. I made eye contact, took a deep breath, and said quietly, "I will help you get your status." She returned my gaze with a serious face. For a moment, she didn't say anything and just looked deeply into my eyes. "This isn't fake. I want to sign a real document and live our lives together. Would this be okay with you?" I asked. My heart was thumping. As soon as I got the words out, I saw she had a little tear forming in the corner of her eyes. Then, I realized how casually it sounded. *How could I talk so easily about such an important issue?* Then, I realized she accepted my strange sort of proposal. Mr. Inoue, the owner of Sushi Ko, kept looking over at us. He might think we have serious problem because Miss Cho was now openly crying. "Yes, but your family is okay? I am Korean," she finally managed to speak. "It's okay, your family is the same too. We will be fine," I assured her confidently. We left the restaurant and I hugged her for the first time. Probably, we are the only couple who didn't even kiss after we decided to marry.

We took a walk around Georgetown just looking around stores, and then we went to the Sheraton near Arlington Cemetery, on top of the hill. The top floor of the Sheraton always had live musicians playing. We sat by the large window in the dining room and could see the shining lights of Washington in its reflection. "Is it okay I don't have money and good job?" I asked, suddenly feeling nervous. "It's okay," she reassured me. "I work hard, and we can get a lot of money later," she promised, smiling. "I have only $8,000 saved. How much you have?" I asked. "Massy, I have only $5,000. I don't care money." She paused, and then added, "but can you give me a Japanese name?" "Okay!" I thought for a minute. "Your name is Eun Soon, and Eun is Japanese pronounced Jun, so I'll call you Jun from now on." "Jun. I like the sound of that!" she answered. "I want to learn Japanese, so can you look for a Japanese language school?" she asked. "Yes, I'll look," I told her. "I also will look for a job, too. I wanted to have my own restaurant someday, but I've never worked at a restaurant before." My future that felt so fuzzy before suddenly came into focus. Although came to the Sheraton to enjoy the music, but we just talked and talked about the life we would build until nearly midnight when the bands were packing up and leaving.

"Yo chan, I am going to get married," I told my brother proudly the next time we spoke on the phone. Always the practical one, my brother collected details about the situation rather than responding emotionally. "What? Who's going to be your wife? When are you going to get married?" I told him, "We've been dating a few months. She's 30 years old, so not too young…" my voice trailed off. "And, she is Korean," I added hastily. "What is going on?" His voice became louder and more stern with each word he spoke. "You know, Aniki, marriage is not easy. Are you sure about this?" "I mean, yeah. She's very nice," I assured him. I knew that no matter how long I'd been here or how clear I was in my decision to stay, that my brother held out hope that I would come back to he and mom in Japan and settle down. He just sounded so disappointed in me every time we spoke. This was supposed to be joyous news, but instead I just felt guilty. I had my own life that was unfolding here in America. After this particular phone call, I felt the connection begin to dwindle with my family and Japan.

Jun and I went to the Arlington Courthouse to submit an application for a marriage license on April 8th, 1980. Afterwards, we went back to Kay's house and shared the news with her. Unlike my brother, she was overjoyed at the news. "I'm so glad for you both, Massy! You two are a great couple! When will you have the wedding?" "No, Kay, we don't have money," I explained. "No money, no wedding." "You don't need money, but you must have wedding! This is the beginning of your shared life together," she urged me. When I looked at Jun, I saw she was smiling and nodding at Kay's words. "Massy, just set the date," Kay said with finality.

That Sunday morning when the Ikard's sat down on the couch to read that week's issues of the *Washington Post* and *New York Times*, I shared my big news. "Mr. and Mrs. Ikard, I am going to get married," I told them enthusiastically. "Congratulations! Is she the Korean girl who went to Martha's Vineyard with you?" Mrs. Ikard wondered. "Yes, Mrs. Ikard." "Massy, when is your wedding?" she asked me. I paused for a second, thinking. "June 8th, Mrs. Ikard," I told her, but I just made up the date because it was exactly two months after the date of our legal union. "I am looking for restaurant job, Mr. Ikard," I added, thinking that they were probably wondering how I would support Jun and myself. I went on. "I've never worked at a restaurant before, but I want to open my own restaurant someday, so I need learn real restaurant operations." "That's a good idea," Mr. Ikard said. "Congratulations to you both."

I called Jun later that afternoon. Since our engagement, she continued to stay at Kay's house and kept the same singing job at Shokudoen. "Jun," I said, "I set our wedding date for June 8th. Is that okay?" "Okay, that's good news but it doesn't give us much time to plan things. I wanted to have a wedding, but I am going to be busy," she said, laughing lightly.

A week later, when I went to Kay's place, she exclaimed, "Massy, you've got a good wife. She is making her wedding dress herself." We walked down the hall to Jun's room and she showed me a long, white dress hanging in the closet. It was simple but classic. I knew Jun would look lovely wearing it. *Wow. She knew we don't have much money, so she made her own dress.* Kay told me she was making handmade wedding invitations, too.

A month later, in May, Mrs. Ikard announced, "Massy, we are going to Martha's Vineyard next week, but you don't have to come with us." "Yes, that's great since I am still looking for a job and apartment," I replied, feeling relieved. "By the way, have you and Jun decided on where to go for your honeymoon?" she asked. "I don't know yet. We may not go anywhere, Mrs. Ikard," I conceded. I didn't want to tell her that we barely had enough money to have a wedding, never mind a honeymoon. "If you like, you can go our house at Martha's Vineyard for your honeymoon," she offered. "We won't be there by the time you have your wedding. We have to stay in Washington for a few events and then Mr. Ikard has to attend a conference in New York." I was not expecting her offer but accepted gladly, knowing how thrilled Jun would be to have a honeymoon. "Thank you Mrs. Ikard for being so good to us. We'd love to have our honeymoon at your place," I grinned.

"Jun," I said over the phone. "More good news. We may be able to go on a honeymoon!" "What! Where are we going?" she sounded happily surprised. "We can go to Martha's Vineyard. Mrs. Ikard told me we can stay at their house there." "How exciting! We had such a good time there before when you brought me and Kay." "Yeah, we did. And we will have a great time this time, just you and me," I said tenderly.

On June 8th, 1980, at noon, we had our wedding at the cozy garden near Kay's townhouse complex in Crystal City. Kay prepared the decorations for the wedding ceremony. I asked my friend Mike, who was a master's student in religion at Catholic University, to serve as our pastor. Jun is protestant, but at the time, I didn't understand the difference between Catholic and Protestant. She didn't mind that I asked Mike since he was a good friend. He also was a fantastic chef who specialized in Chinese foods, so he prepared some special Chinese dishes to bring with him to the wedding. Kay's and Jun's friends came to help us with the food, music, and table settings. Mr. and Mrs. Ikard, the Ward family from Shepherdstown, and many of my friends from Georgetown and GW attended, about 50 people in all, which felt like a lot considering neither of our families or relatives could be there. Jun's simple, flowing white dress looked as beautiful as I had imagined. It was not a fancy wedding, but it felt special to be surrounded by the people who had known me since I stepped foot in America and now were helping me ring in this next phase of my American life. Good friends, good food and drink, a good woman to call mine. It was a memorable night.

My Ford Gran Torino station wagon was still running very smoothly and comfortably on the Delaware Memorial Bridge. From the highest point on the bridge, I could see many ship and boats in the distance. It was one of my favorite landmarks on the drive to Martha's Vineyard. Jun gasped from the passenger's side seat. "Massy, I counted all envelopes and guess how much we received?" "I don't know," I said. "How much?" "$4,500 and three rice cookers, four toasters, and so many dinner plates and silvers!" I was taken back by how generous everyone had been and how special the day had been for us.

When other cars passed, they began to honk their horns. We heard honking all the way through New York. Ward's daughters, Julie and Jill, drew a "Just Married" sign and other drawings with shaving cream on my car. I thought that only happened in movies! At first, we were a little embarrassed of the attention that other drivers gave us, but by the time we came through Delaware and New Jersey, we had fun laughing and tooting our horns in return. We stopped in New York for dinner and drove slowly all night though.

Once we were there, we rested and relaxed until mid-afternoon and went to a nice restaurant at the Harborview Hotel in Edgartown in the evening. The Ikard's house had its own small private beach. After dinner, we sat together on the sand and watched the tiny Chappy ferry boat going and coming. The sky was completely dark by then but lights from the ferry dock and moonlight lit up the sky. We talked about how special the wedding had been and about our dreams for our future. Suddenly remembering something, Jun interrupted our lovey talk. "Massy, I may go to Seattle for the job one month. The manager of the night club called me two or three days ago and offered me three times higher than my job now and will pay for travel costs. What do you think about this?" she asked. "Will you be safe? Are they a trustworthy business?" I knew the money would help us but Seattle was so far away. "I know the place and manager," Jun offered. "They are okay. I'll think a little more about it."

The next day, we drove around the island and went fishing at Jaws bridge. We stopped at a small seafood restaurant in Menemsha, one that we had gone to on our last visit. The older Native American owner was there. "I remember you guys, oh! You got married!" she exclaimed. She smiled and brought us extra food, on the house. I watched her a little as we enjoyed the food and for some reason thought back on my Thanksgiving experiences in the United States. I wondered whether her historical memory was quite different than the version I had come to know. If so, she didn't show it; she radiated warmth and kindness.

We came back to Washington after our four-day honeymoon. Mrs. Ikard told me that we could stay their house until we found an apartment. By the end of August, we got our first apartment and I got job, too. That was a summer of many changes. Our apartment was in Arlington, Virginia, just behind the Marriot Hotel at Key Bridge. It was a decrepit old apartment but was walking distance to my job at Fuji restaurant on M Street in Georgetown and Jun's new Japanese language school at the language center in Georgetown. When we moved in, we promised each other one thing, which was that we would spend as little money as possible to save for our future business. We didn't buy any furniture, and instead, I went to Hechinger's to buy the tools to make us a table. I bought a circular saw and drill, which I thought might come in handy for our future restaurant. It was our first and only table, and it was steady and strong. I didn't know then, but we would go on to have meals at that table for over forty years.

I was excited to begin our new life together but saying farewell to the Ikard's was harder than I thought. On moving day, I shook Mr. Ikard's hand and said to them both, "Mr. and Mrs. Ikard, thank you so much for everything." "Massy, thank you too. If you need something, just call me anytime," Mrs. Ikard said, embracing me. I see Mrs. Ikard's eyes were moist. I had lived with them almost six years! It was very hard to make my way in the UNITED STATES, but the Ikard's gave me the energy to develop my knowledge of American life and showed me the potential my future held.

Made from Scratch: A Recipe for the American Dream

HAGERSTOWN

Fuji was a restaurant that had recently opened. The owner was Mr. Kwan, who had a restaurant in Bangkok, Thailand for ten years. He was young and athletic-looking; his face was tan because he played golf often. I assumed this meant his restaurant business was doing well. There are so many nice golf courses in Bangkok. I had hoped to get a job at Mikado, which was the best one in Washington, but there were no positions available. My first salary was $250.00 per a week. There were two other chefs: Katsui, the chief chef for sushi and kitchen, and Shintani was the kitchen chef. Katsui used to work at Mikado, so I learned many techniques from him.

One day, about three weeks after I started, he warned me, "Hirai san, you might need to look for another job, owner Mr. Kwan may fire you soon." "Why? did he say something about me," I asked. "Yeah, you told him you have three or four years of restaurant experience, but you don't know anything! That's what he told me," Katsui said bluntly. "I told him I had over three years in the food industry— he did not ask me specifically about working in a restaurant," I stammered. *This could be bad. I needed the job to be able to afford our apartment.* That evening, when I was in kitchen, Mr. Kwan came to me and asked, "do you know Mrs. Ikard?" "Yes, she is like my American family," I quickly explained. "Oh my god, she's here with Walter Cronkite. He is very famous person in America." His eyes were wide. "I know him too," I shrugged. "They want to *you* come to fix them Japanese food," he said in wonderment. "Can you go to the sushi bar?" When I went to the sushi bar, Mrs. Ikard greeted me warmly. Mr. Kwan stood nearby, listening intently. "Massy, how are you doing? We miss you at the house! Is everything going well?" "I'm fine, thanks for asking, Mrs. Ikard." "Hi, Massy," Mr. Cronkite chimed in. "Mr. Cronkite, hello! Thank you for coming," I said politely. We made conversation as I prepared their sushi. Mr. Cronkite was talkative. "I like Japanese people, I went to Japan more than ten times, and I just enjoyed myself every time I was there," he shared. "Have you been in Kobe, Mr. Cronkite?" I asked him. "No, unfortunately. I went to so many other cities, even Hiroshima too, but I did not have a chance to go Kobe." He smiled and added, "but, I had nice Kobe steak in Tokyo!" I made some of the original dished I cooked early on for Mr. and Mrs. Ikard, and Katsui made some more sushi for them. They stayed over an hour and ate just about everything we made. When they left the sushi bar, Mr. Kwan quickly came out from the manager's office with a camera. I took picture with them and Katsui took a picture for everybody. Since then, Mr. Kwan was very polite to me, and I never heard another word about getting fired.

All was quiet until the next month when Katsui did not come to the restaurant one morning on a shift he was supposed to work. "What happened to Katsui san?" I asked Shintani. "The owner fired Katsui san," he told me gravely. "Why?" I asked. "I don't know," he said, shaking his head. Katsui is from my generation and is good chef. He is from Kobe too, so we got along well. I called him as soon as I got off work. "Kastui san, what happened?" "I hit Mr. Kwan's son, Jay, in the face. He is just a little boy, but he kept bossing me around. I don't like little ones to order me around. He's not my boss!" he explained angrily. Jay was a nineteen year old college student. Sometimes he came into the kitchen and pushed us around and told us to do things a certain way. I knew that Katsui did not like him, and Katsui had a black belt from a very aggressive karate group in Japan called the Kyokusinkai. Tensions had been brewing for a while, and I guess Katsui finally had enough.

Since then, Shintani moved to the sushi bar and I was the only one in the kitchen. A week later, Mr. Kwan came into the kitchen with a strong-looking man. "This is Mr. Iwasaki," he said, introducing us. "He is a good sushi chef from New York, and he is our chief chef from now on," Mr. Kwan told me firmly. Iwasaki was a quiet man with short hair and narrow, sharp-looking eyes, and a skinny frame.

Shintani and I stuck together and didn't make conversation with Iwasaki much. One night when Shintani and I ate our employee's dinner, which was fixed from whatever leftovers were available from the day, Iwasaki came over and told us, "Oi (hey!) what are you guys eating?! Don't eat junk. Just eat whatever you like, steak, salmon, or anything you like. Don't worry if somebody says something—I said it's okay. You guys work hard and need to eat right." "Are you sure?" Shintani asked, looking dubious. "Yes, it's okay," he said. "Iwasaki san, where did you work before?" I asked him. "I worked at Shinbashi in New York most recently. Before I worked at Tsukiji in Ginza for five years, and I served sushi to Prime Minister Tanaka," he told us proudly. I knew Shinbashi and Tsukiji were both renowned Japanese restaurants in the US and Japan. Shintani and I looked after each other, but we weren't comfortable with Iwasaki. He acted like he had power over the restaurant, but we felt like he was overstepping Mr. Kwan. I don't know every restaurant, but I guessed that there is no restaurant employee's dinner that just uses products meant for customers. "Hirai san, you know Iwasaki always keeps a sake bottle behind the sushi bar. I'm sure he drinks all the time during work," Shintani whispered once Iwasaki walked away. "Plus, he always makes sauces to take home after we leave at night." I started to believe Shintani that maybe we couldn't trust Iwasaki.

I was thinking I would try and find somewhere else to work since I wasn't learning anything new about cooking and had to try and navigate workplace drama. When I explained to Jun about Fuji restaurant's chef and owner, she agreed that I'd be better off at another place. "While you look for another job, I can take the singing job in Seattle for a month, which would help our financial situation," she offered.

So, in December 1980, I took another job in Alexandria, Virginia. A week later, Jun also left for her job in Seattle, Washington. My new workplace, Kyoto, was a new restaurant located on Route 1 in Alexandria, and the owner's name was Nakatsuka. He had come to the US from Osaka and created a small, family-style restaurant specializing in homestyle Japanese foods. Nakatsuka had worked at Sakura restaurant in Silver Spring, Maryland for over ten years before opening his own place. He was a soft-spoken, gentle-looking guy in his late forties.

Suddenly, Jun called Kyoto restaurant a week after she left for Seattle. "Massy, can you pick me up?" She sounded frantic. "Where are you?" "I'm at the airport, the national airport! I came back," Jun explained. "Are you okay? Did something happen?" I was confused. "No, I just can't be separated from you after all," she revealed. I asked Nakatsuka san for permission to leave work and pick up Jun from the airport. "I'm sorry to surprise you like this," Jun explained once in the passenger seat of our car, "but I was not comfortable being so far away from you, so I asked the manager to let me go. He got an airplane ticket for me but told me there was no guarantee I'd get my paycheck since I left early," June mumbled. I could tell she was a little embarrassed about the money but was relieved to be home again.

On Christmas Day, 1980, Jun and I walked around Georgetown, holding hands with each other and looking at the decorated houses and shops like I had done alone for many years. It was wonderful to share the Christmas cheer with someone. I had dreamed about starting my family and laying a foundation down in the US for many years now, and It felt like that dream was starting to fall into place. People were likely home with their families and sitting down to dinner, and the street was quiet. We could hear our footsteps and see our breath in the cold air. I was thinking about my mother and brother in Kobe. Since we married, they did not respond to any phone calls or letters from me. Neither had Jun's family. I realized that an international marriage was not easy for either family, especially since the long-standing rivalry between Korea and Japan. But, I believed that as long as we were happy together and healthy, someday they would understand and accept our union.

New Year's Day, 1981, was right around the corner. "Akemashite Omedetou (Happy New Year!) Massy," Jun said in Japanese. "Akemashite Omedetou, Jun." "I have some happy news to give to you this New Year's Day," she said, smiling broadly. "What? "I asked. "We are going to have a baby!" "When did you go to the doctor's office?" I asked curiously. "No, I haven't been to the doctor's office yet, but I know I'm pregnant." She was so happy. I looked her with wonder and reached out to touch her stomach, but she said, "Massy, what are you doing? It's too early to feel the baby yet!" We both laughed.

The joy of Jun's news didn't last long; I quickly remembered that we didn't have health insurance, so the cost for medical care and delivery was heavy on my mind. I kept running calculations, but every bottom line I ran was one we could not afford. I called Carmen who worked for Mr. and Mrs. Ikard, who helped me before when I needed to change my legal status from a student visa to a green card. I thought she might have some advice for how uninsured families navigated this kind of situation.

"Congratulations, Massy!" Carmen told me over the phone. She listened as I explained my fears about not being able to afford healthcare for Jun and the baby. "Try to contact Providence Hospital," she advised. "They have a program for low-income people who need help. I had two babies there, and I didn't pay anything." I felt hopeful that this would be the case for us, too.

Jun and I went to Providence Hospital the next morning. "From the information you provided, we would charge $1,000 for the doctor and hospital fee, and you could pay that total with minimum payments of $50.00 each month," the wrinkled hospital receptionist said in a gentle voice. She smiled thinly and took us back to the doctor's office.

We looked around the hospital as we walked down the hallway way, and most of the nurses in white uniforms greeted us as we passed. We liked them and left feeling lucky that Jun could get affordable care.

Working at Kyoto was much better than Fuji. The other employees and customers were nice, and the owner was more honest and understanding. The only complaint I had was that the employee meals were much more meager than Fuji. They only let us use vegetables and tofu. I ate tofu almost every day. Kyoto was closed on Mondays, so Jun and I walked around near the apartment building almost every Monday or go visit Kay.

Since Jun got back from Seattle, she hadn't been back to work. So, she started learning how to drive a car. Jun told me she had a driver's license, but she really didn't know how to drive. She told me that the examiner took pity on her and recorded a pass for her test because she was a popular pop singer in Korea. Each day, I gave her driving lessons. She tried to keep busy while I was at work. She went to Japanese language school every day, visited Kay often, and became busy knitting clothes and blankets for the baby. Although Kyoto was better than Fuji, I hadn't learned any new cooking techniques that would help me eventually open my own place.

So, in May, I quit and began working at a restaurant called Nara in Bethesda, Maryland. The owner was an old Japanese man, but he never came to the restaurant. Instead, a met the manager, a younger Japanese man who was the one who hired me. All my coworkers were young too: two were Japanese, two were Thai, and two others were Salvadorians. They made contemporary-style sushi and other Japanese dishes. I wasn't sure what it would be like to work with a bunch of young people as a married man with a baby on the way. But, business was steady, and the style of food was fresh and new.

One night when I came back home from work and opened the apartment door, it was very smoky and smelled like cigarettes. "What's going on, Jun?" I asked her. "Massy, you haven't stopped smoking cigarettes, so I'm going to smoke, too," Jun said crossly. I had been a heavy smoker for long time. Jun asked me stop, but I tried and tried and just could not stop. "Sorry, Jun," I told her earnestly. "I'm going to stop this time, for real!" I threw away all cigarettes from my pockets and from my desk, too. It was very hard. I was smoking between 1-2 packs a day. But, I had to stop because of my first son was in Jun's stomach, and I wanted to do my best as a dad and husband. I still drank a lot of liquor, but thankfully Jun didn't make me quit that, too.

I got a letter from my mother in Kobe in June 1981. *Congratulations!* she wrote. *You will soon be a father! I will visit you soon and would like to meet your wife.* I sent a letter to Kobe when we found out we are expecting a baby, almost a month ago now. "Massy, do you think your Mom will like me?" Jun looked worried. "Don't worry. I know she will," I assured Jun, putting my arms around her.

My mother arrived 10:00 am at Dulles International Airport in June 1981. "Okaasan hajimemashite Jun desu (How do you do mother? I'm Jun.)," Jun said, reaching out for my mom's hand. "Wow, Jun, you can speak Japanese!" Mother was surprised. She asked, "Jun, are you feeling okay? Your belly is getting big now!" She looked at Jun for a while, taking her in, and smiled. "I'm okay, Okaasan, thank you for coming to America," Jun said politely. "Okaasan, is Yochan doing well? Is he still angry with me?" I asked. "Daijyobu (he's okay). He will understand soon, don't worry," Mom said, looking at me. She was not 63 years old, and it had been over five years since I had seen her. She looked different, and I wondered if I did too. I softly put my hand on her shoulder, which felt bony and weak. I broke her gaze and looked down. "I'm sorry, Mom." I was so glad she came to see us. I'm sure it was not easy to make up her mind about visiting us. "I hope she likes me. I'm trying hard," Jun murmured to me in English from the back seat when we left the airport for our apartment. My mother sat in the front passenger seat at Jun's request. This gesture was expected for elder people in Japan."

When Mom walked into the apartment, she commented on how big it was. I had almost forgotten that the average American room is three times bigger than an average Japanese room. "Is this my room? It's too big for only me; in Japan four people could easily sleep here," Mom commented. The next day, Mom, Jun, and I went and walked around Georgetown and then drove to Kalorama Square, so that Mom could thank the Ikards for all they had done to help me over the past five years.

"Glad to see you, Mrs. Hirai," Mrs. Ikard said when she opened the door. "Thank you very much for your special support to my son," Mom said back to her in Japanese. I knew Mrs. Ikard couldn't understand what she was saying, but I think she heard the gratitude in her voice. "Massy is good man. He stayed and worked for us for five years," Mr. Ikard told her slowly. As Mrs. Ikard showed Mom around the house, I had a chance to speak with Mr. Ikard. "Mr. Ikard, I'm glad that my family accepts Jun," I told him. "It's a big relief." "Yes, yes," he said nodding. "It can be an issue… just like the Jews and Palestinians," he added. Mrs. Ikard and Mom returned to the room. "Massy, I have tickets for the Kennedy Center tomorrow. Engelbert Humperdinck is playing. Would you like to take your mother?" Mrs. Ikard asked? "Okaasan, Mrs. Ikard wants to give us tickets for the Engelbert

Humperdinck concert tomorrow," I turned and told her in Japanese. "Would you like to go?" "Oh! I like him, yes!" she smiled widely at Mrs. Ikard. I tried to hide my surprise. I thought there was no way Mom know the British singer.

"Okaasan, do you really like Engelbert Humperdinck?" I asked in the car when we left the Ikard house "I don't know him," she admitted, shrugging. "But this is etiquette. I have to make them happy if they offered for us to go." Jun and I hid our laughter. We had no idea whether Mom would like his style. It was our first time going to the Kennedy Center. There were many people wearing formal evening wear and standing in front of the concert hall. Waiters were busy walking around serving cocktails in addition to the three inside bars serving snack and drinks. I sipped on a Cutty Sark on the rocks. Our seat was in the middle of the third row, which were some of the best seats in the theatre. Tom Jones and Engelbert Humperdinck were some of the biggest stars of the time. The audience was packed and everyone was talking excitedly and waiting for the musicians to come on stage. Suddenly, the melody to "Love is All" started blaring and the crowd went wild. My mom started moving to the music, and I could tell that even if she hadn't known who Engelbert Humperdinck was, she was still having a wonderful time.

I still worked at Nara in Bethesda every day. Nara was closed on Sundays, which made Jun happy because we could go to church together. She called the Japanese embassy to find out where there was a Japanese church in Washington. I went to a Korean church with Jun before, but I did not understand the language and often fell asleep during the sermons. When I lived in Japan, I was not a Christian or even every religious. Most Japanese people are Buddhist, and Buddhism is ingrained in many aspects of our culture. Anyway, at Jun's insistence, we went to a Japanese church in Arlington, Virginia. Reverend Kanagy was the pastor. He had gone on missions in Japan for twenty five years and spoke Japanese fluently. We met some nice people through the church.

My mother and Jun prepared for the new baby. My mother asked me to buy a nice cotton fabric for them at the store. "Jun, my mother is going to make cloth diapers," I told Jun. "I know in Korea they use them too," she nodded. I'm glad Jun and my mother's relationship seemed to be going so well. Jun asked so many questions to Mom about how to make Japanese home-style foods and was learning to sew clothes. Mom responded well to her questions and seemed to appreciate Jun's desire to adapt to our culture. However, our savings account was not doing so well. Nara paid okay, but there was little leftover after paying our bills. I started to look for a site for our own restaurant, thinking that would allow this baby to have the best life. I know a place in Georgetown would do well, plus Jun and I really liked it there, but there's no way we could afford rent or a down payment on a property. I had to keep thinking.

"Hirai san, quickly go home! Okusan (your wife) needs help. I think your baby is coming!" Kaneko, the manager at Nara, shouted across the restaurant on July 8th, 1981. "Sumimasen (I'm sorry)," I answered before rushing home. Of course there was traffic. It took me nearly thirty minutes to get to the apartment. When I got near the entrance of apartment, I saw Jun and Mom were standing and waiting for me with two big bags sitting on the ground. "Daijyobu (Okay) Jun? Just ten or fifteen minutes until we get there," I said to Jun in a car. Her discomfort was growing, and I stepped on the gas pedal. I quickly pulled the car into the emergency entrance at Providence Hospital.

I dropped Jun at the curb and told the people waiting outside, "my wife has a baby coming! I'm going to park the car." "Okay, we'll take care of her, don't worry. Once you park, go straight to the waiting room" an old man told me. Three other people were standing around him, nodding and agreeing. My mother and I sat down in the waiting room. "Men in Japan do not go into the delivery room even if it's his wife," Mother told me. I sat still but wanted to be there with Jun. One hour later, the doctor came into the waiting room and shook my hand. "Mr. Hirai, congratulations! It's a boy!" "Is my wife and the baby okay?" I asked him. "Oh yes," he assured me. "It's a strong boy, 7 lbs. 8 oz, and mother is doing just fine. Soon the nurse will come out and let you know when you can see your wife and baby." "Oh, thank you very much," I said. *I am a father.*

Thirty minutes later, the nurse came out gesturing to me, "I will take you to see the new mom." When we walked down the hall ,I saw so many babies of different skin colors nestled in cribs behind a glass. Many babies had dark skin. Providence Hospital is in the Northeast of Washington, which had mostly Black residents. There were four patients in the room. Jun was the last bed closest to the window and was sleeping. The nurse gave to us two folding chairs and quietly left the room. My mother and I just watch Jun peacefully sleep for a while. "Did you already pick out your baby's name?" Mother quietly asked. "Yes, his name is Kenji," I told her proudly. I thought about boy's names carefully while Jun was still pregnant. I got one word from my father. His name was Sanji; San means upper and Ji means settle. So, Kenji is Ken (build) and the same Ji (settle). Kenji will build the Hirai family that had now settled in the US. I felt it was a strong name with the perfect meaning. "That is a great name," Mom said, patting my hand.

A little while later, the nurse loudly entered the room holding baby Kenji in her arms. "It's visiting time!" Jun woke up, smiled, and made a little space for Kenji beside her in the nook of her arms. Kenji's face was still red from birth and had a full head of black hair that stood straight up. He's what people would call "akachan" in Japanese, which means "red baby." Kenji's eyes were closed, but I said, "Hi Kenji," cupping his head in the palm of my hand. I reached over and held Jun and our baby for a minute, and whispered to her, "Jun, you did so good." She beamed. "I have to call you Otosan (father) from now on," she responded. "Did you settle on the baby's name?" In Japan, traditionally, the father usually picks the baby's name. "Yes, his name is Kenji." "Kenji, Kenji," she said over and over, getting used to the sound of it. "Kenji is just right," she said, looking down at him. I looked at Kenji, so tiny. He looked so much like me with that thick, black hair. "My son, my son," I mouthed, over and over. I could barely believe it.

Jun and Kenji came back to our apartment two days later. I realized how Japanese our home looked. Each bedroom had a futon mattress on the floor. Our room had a large futon and baby futon, side-by-side. There were no bed frames, like many American homes had. Our two bedroom apartment did not have its own washing machine, so Mom kept busy going back and forth to the building's communal laundry room, which was located in the basement, to wash Kenji's cloth diapers. "This machine is very expensive," she complained one day. "What do you mean?" I asked. "I put in four coins, and the dryer just shut off," she explained. I went to the washing room downstairs and discovered that the dryer door's latch was broken, which caused it to shut off prematurely. I fixed the latch, and it seemed to hold fine. "Okaasan, the dryer is okay now." "Okay, but this is an inconvenience anyway, going back and forth, so hopefully soon you and Jun can find another place," she said disapprovingly. I knew we couldn't afford to move right away, so I secretly installed a portable washing machine in the corner of Mom's room. I was pretty good for carpentry and plumbing, and from what I heard, my dad had been a skilled engineer too. We weren't really supposed to do any plumbing or electrical work inside the apartment building, but I didn't want to make things any harder for Mom than I had to. One time, the owners of the apartment had to some in to do some work, so Mom wrapped Kenji in big blanket and stood near the new washing machine to hide it. She must have looked strange just standing still with a baby and a massive blanket, but she kept the secret and didn't even crack a smile while they were there.

Jun and I kept looking for small rental space for our future business. I felt I had enough knowledge by then about how to operate a business after working at three different Japanese restaurants. That weekend, I saw an ad for restaurant space in the *Washington Post's* classified section. The rental was at 25 North Market Street, Frederick Maryland. Frederick was about 50 miles north from where we were in Washington, DC. We all hopped in the car, Mom, Jun, baby Kenji, and me. "It is a very lovely place, not too far from Washington. I like it here, the clean air and vast green fields," Mom commented. "Yes, I like here too, I think we should take this one," Jun told me. Everyone was in agreement.

So, we signed the contract papers a week later. We signed a five year lease agreement. Rent was $2,500 a month, with the first month free and a $2,500 security deposit. Plus, we agreed to 30 days grace time for renovations. Because our apartment in Washington was so far, we rented a place only two or three miles west from downtown Frederick, called Waverley Garden Apartments. "Oh, I do like it here," Mom said again. "And look, we'll even have our own washing machine!" The place we were renting used to be a retail store, so I had to make some changes to both the interior and exterior to make it suitable to use as a restaurant. Some of the renovations we could do ourselves, such as some minor demolition, electrical work, and painting.

However, I was in for a big shock when I went to the city engineer's office for a construction permit the following week. The building we were renting in was a registered historical building, which required us to submit any new building designs to a certified architect. This would cost us thousands of extra dollars. "Jun, we have problem," I explained when I came back from city hall. "What happened?" "I just learned that we'll need a costly special permit because this is a historical building." "Building owner did not mention anything about this to me," she admitted, sounding nervous. "Anyway, we don't have the money for this. We're over our budget as it is," I told her. "I'll go talk to the owner right away," she said, grabbing her purse and jacket from the coat closet. The office was a few blocks away. It was a short trip. Jun was back fifteen minutes later, and her face was pale and she slumped down quietly. I knew right away that there was nothing we could do. I should have researched the building more carefully before we signed the contract. The building owner told Jun, "when you open your own restaurant, you should have enough money to cover expenses like this. Even $10,000 extra is nothing."

Jun and I discussed what our options were. I knew we would have to spend big money for building permissions, and I also knew that more expenses would surely accrue. We just sat together on an old beer carton in the empty dining room, feeling defeated.

The following week, my old friend Ward paid us a visit. He wished us a hearty "Congratulations!" when we opened the door. I had told him on the phone that we had moved to Frederick, so that we could open our own restaurant. "Aw, I'm so happy for you both. Have you picked out a name for the restaurant?" Then he noticed our downcast expressions. "What happened? Did you run into a problem?" he asked. I explained about the historical register issue. It was simply my mistake, I explained. I should have waited until we had more savings. Ward offered to talk with the owner about refunding our security deposit money because it had been only ten days since we signed the lease agreement. He also mentioned that his friend named Sam Leiter was looking for someone to rent his space in Hagerstown.

We did not know where Hagerstown was, but Ward told us that "Hagerstown is the 2nd largest city in state Maryland, only 20 minutes away from Frederick." We decided to quickly move on to Hagerstown and try our luck there instead. Fortunately, when I explained about my new restaurant situation, the apartment manager told us "we understand. Anyway, you did not move into the apartment yet, so we will return your security deposit." We would be able to use that money towards a place in Hagerstown. Ward returned to us later that afternoon with bad news. The building owner did not refund the $2,500 security deposit. She told Word, "I will not return any money because they broke our lease agreement. They are still lucky I did not force them to pay their five year lease payment."

"How do you do? I'm Hilton," said a tall young man who extended his hand to me. He was the owner of the Dagmer Hotel. Ward, his friend Sam Leiter, and I went to Hilton Smith's office two days after our security deposit was declined. Hilton was young, maybe in his late 20's, and very friendly and bright. "So tell me. What kind of restaurant are you making?" he asked, once we all sat down in his office. "I'm Japanese, so I plan to open an authentic Japanese restaurant," I responded. "Good, good. I heard you are from GW. I'm from Georgetown U, so we are both Washingtonian," he smiled. From the first meeting with Hilton, I was already comfortable and at ease with him. Plus, his rent was much more reasonable than the place in Frederick. It would be $950 a month for three years and included utilities. Ward's friend Sam had just signed the lease agreement with Hilton, but the space was not large enough for Sam's new catering business. Hilton was pleased with the arrangement. "This works out well for everyone. Sam is happy, I'm happy, and Massy is happy."

I drove back to our old place in Virginia that night and exclaimed, "Jun, Hagerstown is a pretty nice town! The building owner is a young guy and very honest. And the rent is very cheap!" I had a much better feeling about this place then when I had signed the lease in Frederick. "That is terrific. Did you find us an apartment?" she asked curiously. "Not yet. I'll look for it tomorrow, but Hilton, the new owner, told me we are welcome to use his old apartment above the restaurant with free rent until we find a place." "Really? Wonderful! Little Kenji, we are moving!" she said softly, looking down at him in her arms.

In October 1981, Mr. and Mrs. Nakagaki, Reverend Kanegy from the Japanese church, and my friend Ando from the Kyoto restaurant, helped load our belongings, which weren't much, into all our cars and drove to West Antietam Street in Hagerstown where our restaurant and temporary apartment would be. When we arrived in Hagerstown, Jun looked back into the Reverend's pickup truck bed. "What happened to our tree? Before we left, Mr. Ikard gifted us a six foot high white birch tree." There were no leaves left on the tree, only two or three bare branches. We realized the wind had blown all the leaves away and were afraid the tree would not live.

Everyone helped us unload our things into the storage room behind the restaurant's kitchen. We felt so lucky. The restaurant space had a large area for dining, plus plenty of kitchen equipment: two large refrigerators, a six-burner gas grill, two ovens, and a food warmer. We could save a lot of money. In addition, there was plenty of space for our family in the apartment above the restaurant. Hilton also helped us to apply for a liquor license since the application stated that applicants had to have lived in Washington County for least three years. The Dagmer Hotel was old and was originally used for auto manufacturing in 1920.

I realized that Hagerstown was an important city on the East Coast of America at one time. In the 1980's, there were many companies that had operations in Hagerstown: Fairchild Aircraft

Company, Pangborn Manufacturing, which made military armory products in the first and second world wars, Maryland Ribbon company, the biggest ribbon company in the US at one time, and Tanley Manufacturing, which made leather car seats. Plus the Fort Ritchie army base and Camp David were nearby.

"Masabon," Mom said, using her nickname for me, "is this apartment okay?" She looked worried. There was one cramped elevator for the whole building, with steel bars on the front of it. It could carry four or five people at most. The single light flickered as the elevator started to move up each of the levels. We could smell spoiled food coming from each floor we passed. Hilton had warned me, "my apartment is not a luxury type." I did not pay attention at the time, for all I could think about was that we could live there for free. A few days after we moved into the apartment, I began to understand that this apartment was for low-income and elderly people who needed government help.

Right after we moved in, we encountered a man in the elevator with an amputated left arm. He smelled strongly of alcohol. He looked straight at us and shouted, "I fought for this country! Look at this arm, they took my arm because of you people! I hate you!" I assumed he was a Vietnam war veteran. "Sir, we are Japanese," I tried to explain. "Japanese, Chinese…you're all the same. I hate you. Just look my arm," he shouted again. I just ignored him and stepped slowly in front of Jun. "Otousan, koko kowai (I'm scared here)," Jun murmured. Finally the elevator stopped at the third floor and we shuffled out quickly.

Open House of Kobe

Fortunately, we found a different apartment a week later. Youngstown Apartments was newer than the Dagmer and located in front of Hagerstown Junior College. Jun was relieved, and so was Mom. Knowing that Mom, Jun, and Kenji were in a safe location, I could focus more on the renovations and prepare to open the restaurant.

I wanted to make an entryway, a front desk, and add Japanese decorations in the dining room. I liked to do carpentry and I could use the tools I bought when Jun and I moved into our first place together. I was rushing to be ready before the busy holiday season came. Many of the small jobs I could do myself, but I had to get sub-contractors to take care of the plumbing and complex electrical jobs. We found a plumber who would come out right away. When he was busy connecting some equipment, Jun said loudly to me in English, "I don't trust this man." Jun felt the plumber was taking too much time for an easy job. The heavyset plumber turned to look at me sharply. "Jun, you're speaking English, not Japanese!" I chided her in Japanese. Her face turned beet red. "Ah, we are talking about something else," I tried to explain to the plumber. Jun sometimes confused Japanese and English because she was learning them both at almost the same time. She had lived in the US almost two years, but she was always staying with Koreans, so her English was very poor.

One night when we sat down to eat, I asked in English, "Jun, do you have any cash?" "I have some, but not too much. What do you need it for?" "Money is short after the renovations, and we still have to buy some Japanese dishware so that people can get a real Japanese feeling when they eat," I explained. "What happened?" Mom chimed in in Japanese. "Your faces are serious." She stared at us blankly. "It's okay, Mom, don't worry. We're just talking about money." "If you need some money, I have some," Mom offered. Jun and I looked at each other. "Is it okay if I borrow some? We need to buy dishes for our opening." "Yes, please go ahead and use it." We both thanked her profusely. After a small pause, Jun had an idea: "Otosan, Kay told me a while back that there's a place that has very fair prices for dishes in near Williamsburg, Virginia." So, the next day, we left Hagerstown in the early morning and headed to Williamsburg. My car, the trusty Ford station wagon, purred as it sped up on the highway ramp to I-95 South. Jun enjoyed the drive and treated the trip like a small vacation. Since our honeymoon, we hadn't gone anywhere, just stayed at home or worked. Life with a baby was challenging sometimes, too. We didn't talk much on the way there, just looked at the sights out of our windows and enjoyed the drive. It was very easy to find the place called Williamsburg Pottery Factory—it was as large as a football stadium.

"Jun, you can get some dishes for the home, too, if you like," Mom offered when we got there. "I'm sorry I didn't get anything for your wedding, son, so I hope she picks some nice ones for home," Mom told me in Japanese. We did a lot of shopping and stopped in Georgetown on the way back for dinner. While having dinner, I was thinking about an opening date at our own restaurant. *Now that we have dishes*, I thought, *we might be able to open in the next week, once the kitchen helper, David, completed a little bit more training.* He said he had two years of experience working at a restaurant. It felt strange, but nice, to be hiring people to work at my restaurant rather than applying to work at someone else's place.

We received word from the health department that we were up to code on November 25th. Mr. Kent Hedges, the health department inspector, called me and announced, "Mr. Hirai, you can come to pick up your restaurant permit." He had been kind to me when I filled out the application and shared tips about the food business.

On, November 26th, 1981, House of Kobe opened. I hired three Japanese waitress. They just came to me and asked for a server's job without even seeing the newspaper ad. I guess word had traveled that a Japanese-run business was opening. They were all in their late forties or early fifties. In Japan, we called women like them "sensoh hanayome (war brides)."After the end of the second World War in 1945, there weren't many men left and too many young women and widows. Plus, many American soldiers still occupied Japan especially in Tokyo and Okinawa. Many of the soldiers returned to the US accompanied by young brides. The waitresses wore traditional kimonos, and so did Jun. I imagined it must have been difficult to wear a kimono as a Korean woman, but Jun didn't make any complaints.

At 5:00pm, I turned on the neon "Open" sign at the front door. Jun and I were tense. Suddenly, I felt the weight of the situation. This was my restaurant, and its success or failure would fall to me. We had so much riding on the business doing well. By 6:00pm, no one had come. At 6:30pm, two customers came. At 7:00pm, one more person came. "Hirai san, today is Thanksgiving Day, " one waitress, Mariko, told me gently. I was rushing to open the restaurant as soon as possible and had for-gotten the date. Our bank account balance was dropping lower and lower, so even though it was a mid-week opening, I thought any paycheck was better than nothing.

The next evening, Friday night, we had so many customers come. I was crazy busy, and the kitchen helper David wasn't much help with the meals. I had only taught him how to make tempura, but he could not control the temperature of the wok. So I had to cook every meal and the servers had a hard time keeping the customers happy while I cooked. Jun was the only one who stayed cool and calm. She came back into the kitchen at one point. "Otosan, customers at four table are still waiting for their food. It's been a long time." I know she tried to say this as gently as she could, seeing how busy I was. "I'm sorry. I'm making them one table at a time. Can you give them something in the meantime?" I said frantically. From 5:00pm to 9:00 pm, I made order after order without pause.

Many of the customers that came on opening day still come to House of Kobe today, almost 40 years later. After all the customers left, we had a late dinner with all the employees and my mom and Kenji. I understood how important it was to have dinner together with all the employees after evening business. That way, we could discuss how we did, how the customers felt about the meals, and grow the relationship between workers, so that we felt more like family. We kept up this tradition for twenty years, but eventually we had to stop dinner together because more employees were hired and they had their own schedules and families to get home to. It didn't feel right to keep them away late into the night.

"Jun, David is not a good worker," I told Jun later at home. "Yes, I agree, but he was fast at washing dishes," Jun said. "I think he said, 'I have 2 years of experience working at a restaurant,' but maybe he was just washing dishes?" I wondered out loud. "Maybe so." "Anyway, I'll keep him as a dish washer for a while," I mused. "Everyone needs a chance to learn."

We had steady business over the next month or so, especially on Friday and Saturday nights. But, business started to slow down after that, little by little. I was so tired because I was still cooking every meal we served by myself. The first few months after we opened had gone by in a blink.

Mr. and Mrs. Ikard came to House of Kobe 1 month after we opened. "Massy, this is a fantastic restaurant," Mrs. Ikard grinned, embracing me as soon as she came into the restaurant. I was touched by her words and their presence during the Christmas season. "Aw, thank you, Mrs. Ikard! I'm so glad you and Mr. Ikard came. I know you have so many events to attend this time of year." "Hi! Jun, you look good in a kimono!" Jun greeted them and started to hand menus to the Ikards, but Mrs. Ikard waved it away. "Oh, we don't need a menu. Massy knows what we like!" She winked. "Massy, Walter wanted to come too, but he got tied up, so he asked me to give this to you," she explained, handing me a wrapped picture frame. The picture inside was of a smiling Walter Cronkite with an inscription on the glass that read, "Massy, congratulations! Good luck with your restaurant!" I kept this picture frame near our entrance for many years. "Otosan?" Jun asked when we had gone back into the kitchen. "Do you know what they want?" "Yeah, no problem. They like tempura and Japanese-style veggies," I told her.

Their meal came out quickly, and they started to dig right in. A few minutes later, I could see their eyes scanning the restaurant, so I went right over to them. "Massy, you've never made this salad dressing before for us!" Mrs. Ikard commented. "Is it okay?" "Oh my. This dressing is just superb," she praised. "Making a good salad is the only thing I learned from having worked at three different restaurants before this," I explained to Mrs. Ikard. "I'm glad you enjoyed it." "We have a good friend who owns a sauce company. I can introduce him to you if you want, Massy. I think you have a winner here," she said. They stayed another two hours and then left to go back to Kalorama Square. I thought back about my first few years in America, doing manual labor on their Shepherdstown farm. I was proud that they saw me finish school and now open my own place and was grateful for the support they had shown me as I worked to get to this point.

By the time six months had gone by, we had only ten or fifteen customers on weekdays and twenty to thirty customers on Fridays and Saturdays. But, the customers we did have came often to House of Kobe and were very supportive of me and Jun. Dr. John Marsh was one of our most special customers. He came at least three or four times a week. "Massy, how many people came today?" he'd always ask. Sometimes, I put up only three or four fingers up in response. "Massy, this is meat and potato country. These folks are not seafood lovers," he chortled. "Sensei (doctor), how did you hear about this place?" I asked. "My best friend in medical school was Japanese, and he told me so much about his favorite foods and customs. I became fascinated with learning about your country and was so happy when I learned there was an authentic Japanese place opening around here." I realized our major customer base was full of doctors, lawyers, or other small business owners who had some knowledge of Japan or an open mind when it came to trying new foods.

Dennis Shaw and John Bear were also very special customers of ours, too. Dennis went to Japan when he was child. He showed me his school picture with a Japanese-style elementary school uniform. In Japan, school kids had formal uniforms just like the one he had worn for the photo. When I looked at his picture, it reminded me of my own childhood, and I had a wave of nostalgia come over me. It was the strangest thing. I hadn't missed Japan in a long time. John Bear worked in Japan as an English teacher. He lived in a small countryside city called Takamatsu, which had a famous noodle shop. I had been there a handful of times, long ago.

I hired two Asian boys who had just finished high school and were not interested to attend college. They were much more efficient kitchen helpers than David had been. John Srun was from Cambodia, and Nagc Tran was from Vietnam. David the dishwasher left three months after we opened. Since business was slow, the two new hires would be plenty to keep things running smoothly in the back.

One night in January, Jun came to the kitchen and exclaimed, "Otosan, a Japanese customer came tonight!" "Really? Okay, I will talk to him." I was excited to meet another Japanese person and see how they felt about our food. "Irasshai mase (welcome), Hirai desu (I'm Mr. Hirai)," I introduced myself, using the traditional last name. "Thank you for opening a Japanese restaurant in Hagerstown," he said warmly. "I'm Gene Nakada." "I was very surprised there were more Japanese people in Hagerstown," I admitted. "Maybe you are right. I don't know any other Japanese people here. I can't believe you found a Japanese waitress," Gene exclaimed. He also introduced me to his mother, Daisy, who was 82 years old.

Daisy's story was an interesting one. She told me she came to the US by ship in 1920 as an international student. She arrived in San Francisco, then caught a train bound for Chicago. She was the first Japanese women to attend Chicago University. The only other Japanese student there eventually became Daisy's husband. They were both Christians back in Japan, which was rare. They moved back to Japan after college. Daisy became a schoolteacher and her husband became a pastor and Bible music writer. Despite living in Japan, they only spoke English at home, which they felt would be best for their children's future. During the second world war, Japanese Imperialism cracked down on Christian homes. Gene's father, Ugo Nakada, was taken away many times to an "educational camp", which was really a prison camp. But after the war ended, Junko and Gene, their children, were hired by the US General Headquarters in Tokyo and moved to the US shortly thereafter. Junko moved to California, and Gene moved to Washington DC and joined the US army. He retired from the army in Hagerstown and took a new job at Fairchild Air Craft, and then he became Japanese Specialist for the FBI. He was quite busy during Okinawa's transition from US to Japan ownership. Gene told me he met many of the high-ranking Japanese officials during the transaction, including Japanese Prime Minister Nakasone.

Daisy came back to Hagerstown in 1972 when she retired as a kindergarten teacher in Tokyo and her husband past away. She held a record in the state of Maryland, which was the oldest person to be issued their first driver's license. She was 72 years old. Our families went to Japanese church almost every Sunday together. After a while, as our family grew, we stopped going with the Nakada family and went ourselves every Sunday to attend church and go sightseeing around Georgetown.

Our restaurant specialized in sushi, tempura, and teriyaki, but House of Kobe was still slow. But, I didn't feel especially proud of our fish, which a company delivered to us three times a week. So, one morning, I woke up at 4:00am and left to the fish market in Baltimore's Inner Harbor. My first impression of the fish market was that it was very dirty, old, and crowded. But, I could pick the fish myself rather than having to take whatever was on the delivery truck any given day. It was worth it to squeeze through the crowds because the fish I picked was so fresh. I started to go to the fish market on a regular basis, hoping that having the freshest fish would help improve our business. I usually got back from Baltimore around 10:00am and started to prepare for the lunch shift.

One morning, Mom asked me, "Masabon, I want to see the American fish market. Can you take me?" We went together when the Baltimore Fish Market moved to new location at Jessup, near I-95 and Route 175 just beside the Maryland prison. The new fish market had been modernized and was open to the public. It cost $10.00 each for admission. She browsed the market, slowly moving past each seller's stand and checking out their selections. "Look! They're being so wasteful!" Mom said when she looked at their garbage containers. "Is it okay if we take some fish bones home?" she asked me. There were a lot of fish bones with bits of meat still on them. In Japan, markets like this sold fish bones, too.

"Wow! This soup is mouth watering!" Dr. Marsh said the evening Mom made traditional Japanese soup from the bones we got at the fish market. "Sennsei, every sushi restaurant has this kind soup in Japan. Fish bones makes very tasty soup. Often times, once the bones have been used for soup stock, restaurants sell the fish bones to farmers since it works well as fertilizer." Dr. Marsh looked deep in thought for a minute. "Yeah, I guess we just throw them away here in America," he mused. "We waste a lot of things." "But," he went on, "I feel like in the future more Japanese products and customs will make their way to the US." His prediction came true—more Japanese products were imported in 1980's to 1990's such as automobiles, computers and computer games, foods, fashion, and interior design trends. Many imports were brought in from China, too, the following decade. When I was at GW, I researched automobile marketing in 1975. Japanese cars only made up 4 % of the American markets but would eventually grow to 53% in 2015. Japanese companies began to manufacture and assemble cars here too as the years passed rather than importing already-assembled cars.

My mother left Hagerstown in 1982 because she was not able to extend her visa any longer. She helped a lot, taking care of Kenji and helping us financially when the business started. "Otosan, I think we should move to a bigger place soon," Jun mentioned to me shortly after we left our apartment one morning. "We don't need a bigger place, Jun," I disagreed. "My mother already left and now it's just the three of us again." "Well…I think we might have another baby," she announced. I felt something had been a little different, but I hadn't realized it until she said something. "Is that so?" "Yeah, I'm pretty sure another one is coming," she smiled put her hand on her belly.

So, we began to look for a home to fit our growing family. "How about that one?" Jun suggested, pointing to a sign on the side of the road that read: "Brand new house for sale! Only 1 block away!" We were driving around on Mt. Aetna Road near the Dual Highway. I did respond because I knew we weren't able to afford it. However, already started to collect information about it. Two or three days later, she came to me, excited. "Otosan, the list price is $75,000 but they're willing to sell it for $65,000. Let's just try! If it doesn't work out this time, we'll hold off and just keep looking." Another a week later, Ann Driscal, our real estate agent, called me. "Massy! The bank approved your application." I could not believe that, for I had only $3,000 as a down payment. "Otosan, we got a house! Our first house in the US!" Jun was shrieking with joy. It was a small, two-story house with two bedrooms. Our new address was 131 Catawba Place. Yet another chapter had started for us, and I felt optimistic and full of energy. Since I arrived at Dulles airport in 1974, I only had $700 in my pocket. I knew no one. I had no planned path. Yet here I was, with a beautiful wife, baby. and another on the way, my own business, and now my own house. I felt that the Hirai family was putting down roots and growing in American soil. It was so good to see my wife's happy face and feeling like I could provide what we needed to grow.

Of course, buying a new house required more extra expenses like purchasing kitchen appliances, a washer and dryer, and lawn care items. House of Kobe business was still slow. We kept the same small group of loyal customers that came weekly or bi-weekly. 1982 had just gone by quietly, and a new year began again. We had big snow in January in 1983. A commercial airplane crashed into the Potomac River near Washington National Airport. So many people died in the water near the 14th Street bridge.

When the snow stopped, I went out one morning to begin shoveling the hip-high snow in front of our house. All our neighbors were doing the same thing. I saw two young men shoveling just two houses away from us. I looked more closely and realized they were Middle-Eastern. I smiled at them and waved. "Hi!" They were very friendly. "Where are you guys from?" I asked. "We're from Iran," they told me. I explained them that I had very good friends who were also from Iran, including my best man at our wedding. Our neighbors were business owners like me. They owned a big carpet store and antique business in downtown Hagerstown.

From February to May in 1983, we had some special events at House of Kobe. The first one when the local Gourmet Club chose our place for their evening out. I picked all homestyle Japanese dishes and spread out a large buffet for them. It was our first experience serving more than fifty people at once. When I was a GW student, I would take on catering jobs, but they were for a younger crowd and for people who didn't have a lot of experience with Japanese food. I had made greater volumes of food before, but I knew the expectations from club members would be much higher, so I took my time carefully crafting each dish. Fortunately, they enjoyed the homestyle dinner very much. They asked me to make a short speech about Japan and how I came to end up in Hagerstown.

The second event was a private party at House of Kobe. "Massy, when is your slowest day?" Dr. Faulk had asked me randomly one day when he was eating. "Almost every day is slow," I admitted, "but I think slowest day is Monday." "Okay, well one Monday, I would like to have a party. Maybe forty or fifty people may attend," he said. Dr. Faulk and Mr. Weise, who owned a local kitchen equipment store called H.A. Weise, were throwing the party together. I made the exact same foods I had made two weeks prior for the Gourmet Club, since I had gotten positive feedback. Two weeks after that, House of Kobe was featured in the food section of the *Washington Post*. The article noted, "there is only unique Japanese restaurant in Hagerstown, and the owners are a young Japanese couple." It was only a short write-up, but it brought us a lot of business the following month or two.

In June, we had our second child. This time, it was a girl! I made my first daughter's name "Maki." Her name was made of two parts: Ma means "Real or True or Right" and Ki means "a woman's life." She did not have hair but was very cute and had a strong little voice. It was wonderful to watch my family grow into our new house.

House of Kobe's business was okay, and the two boys I hired in the kitchen were becoming more skilled. In December, I got a letter from Japan. It took me a while to recognize the last name of the sender, Yoshida, but finally I remembered he was my high school friend.

He wrote:

> *Sorry you haven't heard from me in a long time and I'm sending this letter out of the blue. I hope your family and business are fine. I need your help because of my business as a general contractor has been very difficult the past six months. I can't stay in Japan. I need to hide somewhere from an aggressive money lender. I should not have borrowed anything from these kind of places, but I needed quick payment. I thought I could get some from my customers, but the company closed. Please let us go to your place, I'm not expecting to be added to payroll, just enough to eat family for six months or a year. Soon will be the end of 1983,and I fear that if I do not pay the lenders by then, they will send the Yakuza to our house. I have to protect my family from them. Please help us!*

"What did your friend say?" Jun asked, seeing my startled face. "He needs my help. He and his family have to flee Japan. Japanese gang members may soon come to their house to collect debt." I explained the whole situation. Without pause, Jun said what I was thinking. "We've got to help them."

Yoshi, his wife Kazuko, and two little boys came to visit Hagerstown around Christmas time in 1983. He was my good friend in high school. He moved up to architect school and worked for a well-known architect company for a while before opening his own construction company. When I left Japan, he had a successful life. I wondered where it had gone wrong.

"Thank you so much for responding to my letter and helping us get here. I was so scared every time the phone rang or someone knocked at the door," Kazuko told me when they moved into the Colonial Apartments, only one block away from our house. Yoshi nodded, agreeing with his wife. "Thank you. You really helped us when we needed it the most." It had taken some expense to help get them here to the US, but I felt good that I was able to help their family. I was able to get their apartment as a company expense and gave him $200 per a week from my pocket money. Yoshi worked at House of Kobe as a kitchen helper, but he learned how to make Japanese dishes so quickly. They had Christmas dinner with our family since House of Kobe was closed. "We had such a peaceful time. I can't believe how comfortable it was to spend Christmas together," Yoshi told me later.

✦ ✦ ✦

Dr. Marsh came to dine for New Year's Eve dinner. Only 50% of the tables were filled by 7:00pm. "New Year Eve is the busiest day in every restaurant," he commented. "Massy, you should look for another location." "Where we should move?" I asked. He thought carefully. "The best is Dual Highway since there are three or four hotels there." The Dagmer Hotel building was terrible. There was nowhere for people to park, and a lot of drug deals and prostitution happened on the block.

House of Kobe closed for New Year Day, 1984. My mom had come back to the US and was making traditional Japanese New Year's dishes. I invited Dr. and Mrs. Marsh and the Yoshida family to have dinner with us. Kenji was enjoying riding a little, red tricycle in the hallway near the kitchen. He liked to play there since there was a slight decline in the flooring from the kitchen to the dining room and the tricycle would move without much effort. "Mima! Mima! Watch me!" he shouted at Mom. She smiled and watched him slide down the hall. Dr. Marsh enjoyed the traditional dishes we prepared. The first three days of the New Year, we didn't eat any four-legged animal meats, but we had fish, chicken, and different types of vegetables. "Hirai san, the flower shop owner Mr. Brown may sell his property. You should try and stop by," Gene Nakada's mother Daisy told me in January 1984. The flower shop, named B & L Garden Center, was located on Dual Highway where Dr. Marsh suggested we relocate House of Kobe. I wasn't really interested in checking it out because my financial situation wasn't strong enough to purchase it. It would be nearly impossible. "How was your talk with Mr. Brown?" Daisy asked a few weeks later. "I'm sorry but I did not have a chance to talk to him yet." I could tell she wasn't satisfied with my response and was just trying to help.

I went to the flower shop the following week and asked to speak with Mr. Brown. After I greeted him, I explained why I was there. "My name is Massy, I have a restaurant in downtown, and I'm looking for new location. Someone told me that you may move to North Carolina and may be looking to tell the shop." "Yes," Mr. Brown responded. "It's true I'm thinking to go back my home in North Carolina, but I cannot decide this on my own. I have a partner, Mr. Leather, that you should speak to about this.

The next day, I went to visit Mr. Leather at his home on Little Antietam Road near Route 60, Leitersburg Pike. Mr. Leather was working in his garage, which had been converted to a small vegetable shop. He was a skinny old man with a soft voice. Once I told him that I had spoken to Mr. Brown about purchasing the flower shop, I could tell he might be persuaded. "Okay, Massy, let me talk with my wife and I'll get back to you about this." He gave me a sack of potatoes before I left. "These are fresh from my garden. I just picked them up this morning" he said kindly. I was very comfortable with him when I left, but I knew getting the bank's approval to buy the property on Dual Highway would still be too difficult.

When I came back to home and told Jun how nice Mr. Leather was, Jun pleaded, "Otosan, please just try to buy the shop." "I know we need to move to a better location, and Dual Highway is the best. But I just don't think we can afford it." "Just try!" "We would have to sell our new house! This is a minimum condition. Is it okay with you?" I looked her and said. She didn't say anything for a few moments. I know she loved our house and wouldn't want to move back to apartment life again. "Okay, I'll give up our house," she said sadly.

Two or three days later, Mr. Brown called me and asked me to stop by his place. "Leather has agreed to sell the property, and the price is $70,000 for property and $20,000 for the business," he offered. I was very surprised the price was so cheap. I thought I'd easily be looking at spending $100,000. I learned that B & L Garden Center business was Mr. Brown's alone. It used to be partnership, but Mr. Leather left the business. From the sale, Mr. Leather would get only $35,000 and Mr. Brown would get an extra $20,000.

My next stop was the bank. "Mr. Hirai, your House of Kobe income for the past three years is almost nothing, and you have almost no personal savings," said Mr. Ed Kemmet, a loan officer at Hagerstown Trust. "Based on this information, it is unlikely that you will be approved for a loan." "We need a new location. If we move to the Dual Highway, our earnings will be much higher," I tried to explain. "I understand. Your proposal statement is very strong, so I will bring your case up at the next board meeting," he responded. The new location was right in between three major hotels: The Holiday Inn, Ramada Inn, and Best Western, plus there was a Sheraton and Quality Inn nearby. I knew that if we could get approved, the business would have a much better chance.

Even though the sales price was $90,000, I applied for a $200,000 loan. We would need the extra funds to convert the flower shop into a restaurant and purchase kitchen equipment and furniture. The B & L Garden Center used to be an old gas station before, so it would likely need quite a lot of work.

"Otosan, it has been already three weeks," Jun said impatiently. "When will we know?" I knew the board meeting for our loan application should have taken place over two weeks ago now. I didn't know whether I should call Mr. Kemmet or not, but I did not call as I did not want to seem desperate. In the meantime, our house got an offer of $75,000.

Yoshi came to me a few days later. "Hirai kun, I heard House of Kobe is moving to the East side of Hagerstown?" "Hopefully so. We need to move to a better location," I confirmed. "If you need some renovations done, don't forget I am here," Yoshi offered. It had slipped my mind that used to be a professional contractor for new construction. *What a coincidence it was that we had an architect and carpenter specializing in Japanese-style buildings!* I thought. "I'd like to do something in my field and not cook tempura at the restaurant," Yoshi added. If the loan was approved, I knew I would take him up on the offer.

Another a week later, Mr. Kemmet called. "Mr. Hirai, your application has been approved." "Mr. Kemmet, you will give us the money?" I could barely believe it. "Yes, but there is one condition, which is opening your business account from your other bank to ours," he explained. Jun was standing near the phone, eager to hear the news. I covered the phone receiver and whispered happily, "Jun, Hagerstown Trust will lend us the money." Much later, Mr. Kemmet told me, "I thought that was no way to approve your application, but my boss pushed for the board to approve lending for House of Kobe," I asked him who had helped us, but he did not tell me.

The settlement was held at Mr. Russel Robinson's office in October of 1984. "Massy, we are so lucky to be able to relocate House of Kobe to the Dual Highway," Jun said at the dinner table after we signed all the documents for our new property. "Yeah, Jun, we are so lucky!" I said. "And I have another piece of good news…" "Baby # 3 is coming!" *Yes, I'm lucky. My family is growing!* I said to myself.

Yoshi was busy drawing up plans for the new House of Kobe building. He designed and drew all specifications for the floor plan and submitted them to the Hagerstown city engineer and Washington County Health Department. Once all the applications had been approved, we started construction in late summer. It was very difficult to add on to an existing concrete building, especially one that was an old gas station. The best way was to demolish the old building and start from scratch, but the cost of demolition was so expensive. I worked hard doing some of the carpentry during the daytime and then went to work at House of Kobe in the evening time every day. On Sundays, when we were closed, I worked at the construction site all day. I had to save any extra expenses during construction because I knew we'd need a lot of items for the transition to the Dual Highway location including kitchen equipment, dining tables and chairs, and more dishes.

During the construction, Reverend Kanagy from the Washington Japanese Church came to help us. He had retired after spending 23 years in Japan on a mission trip and opened a Dutch restaurant in Fairfax, Virginia for five years. Then, he began to help the Japanese church, retired again, and moved back his home to Bellville, Pennsylvania, which was one hour away from Hagerstown. "I was a carpenter when I was young, just like Jesus," he always said. He brought his cousins and friends for our House of Kobe project. They worked very hard putting up the drywall and painting.

Finally, after months of hard work, the new House of Kobe had its Grand Opening on May 8th, 1985. I invited the Mayor of Hagerstown, Steve Sager, to cut the ribbon. Jun wore a Japanese kimono and I wore a white tuxedo for the occasion. Jun had a third baby only one week prior, on April 27th. I named him Seiji. One month later, Jun and I celebrated our 5th wedding anniversary on June 8th. This was one of the happiest periods of my life. In the five years of our life together, we had three beautiful children and owned a brand new restaurant.

We made the restaurant beautiful. Yoshi and I discussed so many options for making a traditional, Japanese-style restaurant. The new sushi bar countertop had four-inch thick solid walnut wood that was twelve feet long. I ordered it from Cavetown Planing Mill. We had a traditional tatami mattress room, where everybody would take their shoes off when entering the room and sit on woven Igusa mats.

The only downside was our housing situation. We sold our house and moved to a three-bedroom apartment across the street from the restaurant in a complex called Town House Manor Apartments. But, we were so happy about the new restaurant that we didn't mind too much.

"Wow! I like here! Look Mom and Dad! I can ride my bicycle!" Kenji announced to us. He was four years old and enjoyed playing in our parking area. Maki was two years old and she was riding her tricycle, too. "Be careful! Only five more minutes!" Jun told them loudly. She was holding newborn baby Seiji. Our first lunch shift was about to start.

It was good to have House of Kobe up and running again. I hired our first Japanese sushi chef named Kato. He specialized in Kappo, Japanese formal dishes. I was lucky to have him, and I learned so many techniques from him too. He would have done well as a chef in a big city like New York or Washington. However, Kato loved his horse and needed someplace with plenty of open space. He bought a farm in Boonsboro and needed work nearby, so that he could still take care of the animal. In addition to Kato, we had John, a young Cambodian who worked at the sushi bar with me, and Houng, who was Vietnamese, to work in the kitchen. I also hired many Korean women as servers. Many of the Korean women were wives of Army soldiers up at Fort Ritchie. The move paid off—business tripled what it had done before in no time. "Massy, I'm so glad you were able to move here," Dr. Marsh told me when he came in and saw how busy we were. He still came in two or three times a week and enjoyed the food and a nice chat with me.

A few months after we opened, Yoshi came to me with news. "Hirai kun, I am going back to Japan." I knew he wasn't happy working at the restaurant especially now that the new House of Kobe building was complete. "Is it okay? Is it safe for you and your family to go back to Japan?" I asked him.

"I think we should be okay. I already contacted an architect's office in Osaka, and I felt they would hire me. Anyway, I am not going back to Kobe, so it's going to be okay," he assured me.

He and his family left Hagerstown in the summer of 1985. "Thank you Yoshi! Without you, I could not survive," I told him. "Thank you, too. This was a good experience and was good for my children's education to be in American schools for a year." I still find it incredible that Yoshi came just at the right time and had the skillset I really needed during our transition. I probably saved over $100,000 building the new House of Kobe thanks to

Yoshi. I got a letter from Yoshi that December telling me that his new office is very comfortable, and his family was safe and happy. He would keep working there, he explained, and never try and start his own business again.

From there, time seemed to pass more quickly. We were doing a great business, but the expenses at the new place were so high. We were earning just enough to pay food costs and the employees' payrolls. I was busy from early morning to late at night, going to fish market every other day at the crack of dawn and working at the restaurant six days a week. But when I came back home, I found that my children waited up for me most nights of the week. Seeing their happy faces helped keep me going even though the days were long.

In Spring of 1987, I began to feel uncomfortable and discovered a hard nodule on my shoulder near my neck. I showed the lump to Dr. Marsh. "Massy, you still don't have insurance?" he asked one evening when he came for dinner. "No, I don't have any yet," said tentatively. "Massy, you should get health insurance now, not just for you, but also for your family. Your kids are still little and you've got to think of Jun too. You never know what happens in the future, you know?" I nodded. "Anyway, for now, just come to my clinic tomorrow," he offered.

I went to Hagerstown Surgical Clinic on North Potomac Street at 3:00pm the next afternoon. "The hospital is better, but here is okay too—and free, Massy," Dr. Marsh smiled and said. I sat down on one of the office chairs and watched what he was doing. He start to cut my lower neck where the skin was raised. I did not feel anything. He talked about many things and used a calming voice. I knew he was trying to put me at ease. "Maybe this surgery knife is very sharp? I don't feel anything," I told him. "Massy, the sharpest knife is a razor blade and second is a scalpel," he explained while he was cutting my tissue and preparing to take out the lump. He was still hard at work on my neck, and I could see sweat beads forming on his forehead. A few minutes later, he removed a lump of dark tissue from my neck the size of a ping pong ball. Once he closed the wound, he told me, "Okay, I took out everything." "Do you know what it is?" I asked him nervously. "I hope it'll be okay, Massy. I'll send this out to the lab and call you tomorrow."

"Is everything okay?" Jun asked when I came back home that afternoon. "I hope so. Dr. Marsh will call me tomorrow and let me know," I said, trying to sound casual. From Dr. Marsh's reaction right after the surgery, I wasn't so sure. I had a sinking feeling that it was something serious. It was the first time I thought about my own mortality. My children were still too little: Kenji was six, Maki was four, and Seiji was only two years old. I prayed to God, "please give to me at least ten more years of life for my family. My children are still too small, and I have so many things I want to teach them." Two days later, my prayer was answered. Mrs. Marsh called and gave me the good news. "Massy, the lab results were negative!" I was so happy. "Can you see the bright sunrise?" she asked. That phrasing felt just right to me, and it was true! My heart suddenly felt really light and bright like sunshine. "Jun, I'm okay!" I told her when I got off the phone. Her eyes were damp but her face suddenly looked as relieved as I felt inside.

Another two days later, when Dr. Marsh came to House of Kobe, he advised me, "Massy, you don't have cancer, but you should see the lymph specialist when you have health insurance, just to make sure everything else is okay."

Thankfully, 1987 had gone by quietly without any other disturbances. The business was still doing well but we were barely able to cover our monthly expenses. When 1988 began, two of our regular sushi customers, Dr. and Mrs. Laurence Hill came in. They were both Black and from Boston. Dr. Hill was a radiation doctor in town. At the end of their meal, they made me an unexpected offer. "Massy, this is a very good Japanese restaurant. It looks great, the food is good, and I know business is going to grow." "Thank you," I told Dr. Hill, not knowing exactly where the conversation was headed. "If you want, I can buy this restaurant, so you can concentrate on making the food, and I would pay whatever you are earning now and you'd have less headache," he said smoothly.

"Jun, Dr. Hill wants to buy our restaurant," I told her later that evening. "If you sell House of Kobe, it will not be yours anymore," she reminded me. The Hills had invited us to their house for lunch that Sunday to discuss their offer more.

Even though I loved having my own business, I was thinking more about how hard I had worked every day for the past seven years. I wanted to have my own time with the family, especially with my kids. I was seriously considering their offer.

But a week after we visited their house, they had a serious car accident. Dr. Hill died instantly, and Mrs. Hill died at home three days after she was released from the hospital.

I don't understand human life. It was so hard to get this news and reminded me of how fragile life is. Only a week ago, Dr. Hill was talking with me excitedly about the future of House of Kobe. A week later, he and his lovely wife were just…gone. *You never know what is going to happen tomorrow. Day by day, I should just do the best I can do for my family.*

Time for Family

In October 1988, I took my family on a ten-day visit to Japan. I was longing to show my home country to my family now that the children were growing older. Jun had never visited Japan either! I had spent over a decade here in the US, and all of a sudden, I was really missing Japan. I wanted to see how Japan changed since my departure in 1974. I knew their economy was rapidly growing. My kids were so excited to fly on an airplane. It was their first experience flying. At first, they were filled with joy, pointing out the small airplane windows and grinning when the plane lifted off the runway. But, soon, the excitement wore off and they were bored and squirming in their seats. It was a fifteen hour flight. They perked up again slightly when the airline attendant came and served each of the three meals. But, once they had eaten, there was nowhere for them to get out their energy and nothing to keep them occupied, for there were no movie channels or gaming devices in those days. All we could do was try to sleep until we arrived in Japan.

After a long flight, we finally heard the announcement: "We are now the position for landing Narita International Airport." I looked down from the window, and I could see dark, rich-looking soil, maybe vegetable fields, divided in small sections representing each farmer's property. I don't know why, but I felt suddenly at ease just staring at the ground below. *Maybe this land is my home?* My children got excited again, watching the airplanes landing on the runway.

It was my first time arriving at Narita Airport. When I left Japan in 1974, it was Haneda Airport as part of the Tokyo International Airport. The Narita Airport was huge and modern. The toilets in the airport restrooms a bidet function and temperature-control seats. Once we left the airport, we went to the old cities of Kyoto and Nara. We also spent three days in Tokyo. Everyone enjoyed seeing the people and exploring the places we went. "Daddy, everyone looks the same in Japan," the kids remarked. I could see what they were saying. Everyone dressed similarly: men wore all dark-colored suits and there was little variation in height or size for full-grown people. We stayed at my brother's house in Kobe. His house was a narrow, three-story house. Japan does not have space for large houses and gardens. Their stairs were steep, more than 45 degree angles, and each step was short and narrow. My family marveled at the Japanese bathtubs, which were also narrow but quite deep. There was no shower. We mostly hand-bathed during our visit. Overall, it was a wonderful trip, and I think out of the five of us, I enjoyed my time there the most. So much had changed in a decade. Japan's way of life, economics, and people's mindsets were changing.

It was a nice break, but we were soon back to real life in Hagerstown. In December 1988, we moved to the house where Daisy had lived. Gene Nakada told me, "Hirai san, if you would like to live in my mother's house, please let me know. The house is not big, but I think it's better than an apartment especially with three kids." By this time, Daisy was 92 years old, and he was worried about her living on her own, so he pushed her to move into his house on the same property. I asked Jun about this option after work one night. "Jun, Nakada san has offered for our family move to Daisy's house, with very low rent. What do you think?" "Yes, let's do it. The children need to play in a yard," she agreed quickly. So we packed up again and moved into Nakada san's small house.

Business at House of Kobe stayed relatively the same in 1988 and 1989. I was constantly thinking about ways that we could grow the business. We continued to have a base of regular customers come several times a week, but we weren't attracting new customers. Most of the people in the area were still not open to trying a lot of Japanese foods yet. The average townsperson probably thought that Japanese foods equal raw fish and very strange foods. As far as I could see, we needed to diversify our menu for those weren't as adventurous. We had to serve meat. This was meat and potatoes country.

I had to think about starting to make Teppan Yaki meals. Rocky Aoki made this style of food a great success in Japanese in the late 1960's. His restaurant called Benihana had come to the US and become something of a phenomenon. Aoki created a Benihana school in Texas because he needed many more chefs to open new Benihana restaurants. My only concern was having the capital, for making a Teppan Yaki table would cost a lot of money. I talked with the loan officer of Hagerstown Trust. "Mr. Hirai, I don't think that we can help you with the new addition because your business situation is not strong enough for a new challenge," Mr. Kemmet explained gently. I knew the bank wouldn't give me money this time. I was frustrated. I knew we needed this for House of Kobe's future.

"Massy, how are you?" Mrs. Ikard's voice came over the telephone. It was summer of 1990. "Oh, Mrs. Ikard, I'm fine. The children are growing fast. How are you and Mr. Ikard?" "Well, we moved. We're still in Kalorama Square, but our new unit has a bigger garden and swimming pool beside the house. Why don't you come here? The kids will have fun swimming," she offered. So we went to Kalorama Square to visit the Ikards the following Sunday. It was very good see them. I hadn't seen them since 1983 when they came to visit us at the old House of Kobe location. They were getting old. Mr. Ikard looked frail, but he was still working at a law farm in Washington, DC. The kids did indeed enjoy swimming in the pool, and we all caught up over lunch and had a great conversation.

Mom called me and announced, "I'm coming to America for Christmas." She had come to the US now three or four times since the children had been born. She really loved her grandchildren, especially Kenji. I often remembered back to when Kenji was born and Mom came to stay with us. At the time, we were so poor. Without her help, there's no way that we could have opened and operated House of Kobe. We picked her up at Dulles Airport on December 22nd, 1990.

Mima, which is what the children called Mom, busied herself in the kitchen most of Christmas Day, making special Japanese dishes for dinner. "This is your Christmas present," Mima said during our dinner, handing me a thick, white envelope. When I opened it, I was in shock. It was all cash, both US dollars bills and some Japanese currency. "There's just about $10,000 there," mom explained "About $6,000 was what you gave to me when you left Japan. I did not use it. I think this time you need it for your business," she added. I remembered when I left Hanshin Company in 1974, I got an early retirement check, and I gave to Mom. "Okasan, that money was for you. You should keep it," I tried to insist. "No, no. I have enough money, and I did not need the money you gave me. I just wanted to use it for something good, so it has a purpose. There's no point in it just sitting in a safe," she said firmly.

It was big help. I now had the money I needed to make hibachi tables. I started the hibachi project from 1991. Yoshi taught me so many tips for renovating a building when the new House of Kobe was built, so I felt much more capable adding the new hibachi area.

In May 1991, I got a phone call during dinner time. "Are you Massy?" "Yes, this is he." "This is Mr. Ikard's secretary, Linda. Mr. Ikard passed away this afternoon. I just wanted to let you know that the funeral will be on Friday. I'm very sorry to call you with this news." I felt in shock, like a giant star had fallen out of the sky. "Thank you for letting me know," I managed to say. Mr. Ikard had been my first American man and had helped me so much over the years. I remembered something when Mrs. Ikard had lunch with her friends at Kalorama Square in 1977. When I serve lunch for them, I heard Mrs. Brooks, Senator Edward Brooks' mother, say, "Jayne would be a great first lady." I'm sure they were talking about Mr. Ikard's future. I didn't know much about Mr. Ikard's political vision, but I agreed that he was a great leader and the type of person most people aspired to be. He made all kinds of people feel so comfortable in his presence and never became emotional or engaged in conflict in front of others. I could not attend his funeral, but later I visited his tomb at Arlington National Cemetery where he was laid to rest.

The end of 1991, I finally finished adding four new hibachi tables in our dining room. I hired a Japanese hibachi chef named Sato. We had much more business once we began offering hibachi meals. I also had John learn how to make hibachi dishes. Making hibachi meals is very simple, but hibachi is not just fixing the meal; all the customers expected to be entertained well when their food was cooking. Fortunately, John picked up on the hibachi-making techniques quickly. He didn't want to go to college and instead wanted to invest his time learning the restaurant business.

Beginning in 1992, I would play golf with John while we took our lunch break between 2:30pm to 4:00pm. There was just enough time to play nine holes at the municipal golf course right across the street from House of Kobe. I had never played golf once in the US since I came in 1974. Playing golf is more of a social event in Japan. Most of the courses in Japan are membership only, and public courses are very expensive. One game might cost upwards of three hundred dollars, so I had only gone a few times in Japan. Here, it was much more affordable, so I really was able to enjoy golf as a hobby. Watching that small, white ball fly over 250 yards felt like such a rush. Once in a while, on Sundays when House of Kobe was closed, we'd play eighteen holes at Black Rock Golf Course, which was only a few miles down the road. In 1992 and 1993, the hibachi tables continued to draw in new customers who didn't know much about Japanese food. People really seemed to love having the chefs cook meat and vegetables in front of them. I also made a new sauce for the hibachi meals called Kobe sauce. Most hibachi restaurants in the US only offered two sauces, usually a mustard sauce and a ginger-based sauce. Having another sauce that people could drizzle on their hibachi meals also helped us expand our customer base. More people began to come from Chambersburg and Waynesboro Pennsylvania, Martinsburg, Charles Town, and Harpers Ferry, West Virginia, and Frederick, Maryland. By this time, about 30% customers were from Frederick.

In 1992, we moved again. This house wasn't too far, just next to Nakada san's house, but was much larger. It was a one-story house with four bedrooms and a large living room on a one-acre lot. It was the first time that each of my children had their own room. Kenji took the largest of the bedrooms, but Maki and Seiji were still happy.

Jun and I began to focus more on making memories with the kids as they got older and taking more family trips together. So we had many good short trips from 1993 to 1998. I especially enjoyed our trips to The Homestead Resort, in Hot Springs, Virginia, the Christmas of 1993. "Dad, is that special drink?" Kenji asked me when the waitstaff placed a small bowl in front of Seiji. "Seiji, don't drink that," I explained. "That is finger bowl, so after dinner people can clean their fingers." "Daddy, it is pretty— and look! There are lemons in the bowl, too!" little Seiji said happily. I laughed. It was our first formal American dinner. I looked at Jun across the table and her eyes were twinkling and she looked carefree. It was at that moment I knew we had done a really good job building our family.

Men wore jackets with ties, women wore cocktail dress, and there was a live band playing in the dining room. Jun and I danced together and the kids watched us, mesmerized. It was the first time we had danced together since our wedding. "Seiji, come with me," Maki told him, tugging on his hand. "No! I don't want to dance," Seiji pouted. But, Maki, who was 10 years old, won Seiji over eventually, and they both laughed and twirled around the dance floor. Maki was smiling and enjoying herself, and Seiji, who was a little more shy, even enjoyed himself. Jun and I stopped dancing, so that we could watch them. Homestead had its also own ski slopes, too. The kids were so quick to master skiing, and it soon became one of our favorite family activities. That trip to Homestead was one of my favorite memories from when the children were young. We got sad news in 1994. Dr. Marsh, who by now was a dear friend, was diagnosed with cancer. When our business was very slow, he always came to House of Kobe at least two or three times a week and was so encouraging to us. It was really his advice that gave us the idea to move locations to the Dual Highway. We went to his farm in Fairplay many times. When his sheep had babies, all my kids would go over and hold the fluffy, white lambs. "Massy, I knew it would happen because I've smoked since I turned twelve years old," he confided in me.

On January 17th, 1995, Kobe had a 7.8 magnitude earthquake. I called my mother but could not get a hold of her for three days due to the phone lines being down. I was so worried something had happened to her. I was watching the news and saw that more than half of whole city of Kobe had been destroyed, impacting 1.2 million people. "Okaasan, are you okay?" I asked frantically when I finally spoke with her. "Is the house okay?" "I'm okay, but the house is damaged. Half our roof is gone," she told me sadly. "I'll be there right away," I assured her. Before

I purchased the ticket, I was thinking about Dr. Marsh and whether he could go with me or not. He always told me how much he wanted to go to Japan, and I wanted show him my hometown Kobe despite the earthquake's destruction. I didn't know how much time he had left. "Dr. Marsh just finished chemotherapy treatment and is weak," Jun reminded me. "I don't think it's a good idea to go to Japan together this time." She was right, I knew.

I was so surprised to see the real scene happening in the town of Kobe. All the buildings, train routes, and highways are located in the narrow strip between mountains and ocean. I saw that the earthquake had caused many landslides to come down from the mountains. Mountains that used to be a lush, green color were now muddy and brown. Houses everywhere had collapsed. There was rubble everywhere. I was glad my mother was okay. She had little hurt her right leg. When the shaking started, she tried quickly leave out of the house and hit her leg on the door. Thankfully, my brother already covered the roof in vinyl, so they could live and sleep in the house until the roof was prepared. They were some of the lucky ones. I heard so many people had to stay in temporary shelters and had lost most of their belongings. What was incredible to me was how everyone pitched in to help one another. The local government sent in food and there were many volunteers who came to help with cleanup from other cities in Japan. All the neighbors checked on one another. Some brought grill tables into the street and cooked foods especially hot soup since it was cold in January. "Masabon, this reminds me of right after the great war. We had nothing, but people took care of one another," Mom recalled. I wondered whether it would be the same in America if the same thing had happened there. I was glad to be there to help, and I knew that with the outpouring of love and care, that Kobe would rebuild in time and thrive once again.

Dr. Marsh died shortly after I came back from Japan. He was such a special person to me. At his funeral, I cried when I hugged Dr. Marsh's brother. He looked exactly the same as Dr. Marsh. I had no idea Dr. Marsh had a brother who lived in Baltimore.

Made from Scratch: A Recipe for the American Dream

FIRE AND IMMIGRATION

In summertime, I started to build another House of Kobe in Frederick. There weren't any Japanese restaurants in Frederick, so many people traveled to eat at the House of Kobe in Hagerstown, which was twenty-five minutes away. If somebody were to open a Japanese restaurant in Frederick, I estimated that we'd lose a good portion of our business. So, I thought I would try and be the first one to open a business there and try and replicate the success we had in Hagerstown. I could be wrong, but I was young physically and mentally and was ready to take on the risk without thinking too deeply about it. Looking back, maybe I was a bit overconfident. The new location was 1507 West Patrick Street, in a small shopping center only three blocks west of the Golden Mile, which was the main road that led into Downtown Frederick. The best location was directly on the Golden Mile, but there wasn't any place available that we could afford. The building owner was Leon Landis, a Greek man, and gave us three months of free rent when we signed a ten year lease.

I had been very busy again as a contractor for the new location. It took about three months of renovations to the existing building before we could open. Opening wasn't as easy because of the Frederick Health Department. They required that the chefs wore sneeze guards around the hibachi grill. The health department officer told me sternly, "Mr. Hirai, I know you have a hibachi restaurant in Hagerstown, but here in Frederick county, we have our own rules. Please think about serving cafeteria style; otherwise we must require sneeze guards when you serve directly to the customers." I tried to explain the drawbacks to him. "It is very difficult to serve from the chefs to the customers if there is a barrier in between them." "I was thinking there ought to be a foot-high wall between the customers, but maybe I might be able to accept a six-inch barrier," he suggested. I almost tried to explain how pointless that would be since the particles from a sneeze or cough move through the air regardless of whether there's a six-inch barrier or not, but I knew he would not agree with me. I showed him many pictures of other Japanese hibachi restaurants in the US that did not have any such sneeze guard. But, I was told that they didn't care what other states did. They were going to follow their manuals. Finally, we opened in October 1995 with our six-inch high sneeze guard around the hibachi table.

It was very busy at the new Frederick restaurant. I was spread thin, working at both the Hagerstown and Frederick restaurant.

At the end of January 1996, something unbelievable happened. The phone rang at 6:00am. "Are you the owner of House of Kobe?" a voice asked. "Yes, I am." "This is the Hagerstown Fire Department. House of Kobe burned down this morning. Please come here as soon as possible." I just sat there with the phone in my hand after the call ended. "What happened?" Jun asked, concerned. "There was a fire at House of Kobe," I told her in disbelief and quickly changed clothes and set out to survey the damage. At the corner of Eastern Boulevard and Dual Highway, a policeman was standing and directing traffic. "You cannot go to Dual Highway," he told me as I rolled down my window, "House of Kobe was on fire this morning." "I'm the owner of the restaurant," I protested. "Okay, please go slowly as there are many vehicles there," he said. It was a shocking scene. There were only some concrete blocks and some charred kitchen equipment still standing. Everything else was a pile of black, smoking ash.

All I could do was stand at the edge of the parking lot and stare at the remnants of the building Yoshi and I had carefully and meticulously designed and built. "I'm Fire Marshal Harsh," said a stocky man with sharp-looking eyes and white hair. "We've been calling you since 4:00am this morning, but you never answered. What happened?" he asked sternly. I heard the Fire Marshal's voice, but I couldn't take my eyes off of the huge piles of ash, nearly two or three large dump truck's worth. I was having a hard time adjusting to reality. Just yesterday there was a beautiful restaurant building there, complete with an entrance, sushi bar, private tatami room, and hibachi tables. I had invested so much time and all of our money making it perfect. I muttered, "Sorry, I was thinking too much. I didn't keep the phone beside my bed, so I didn't hear your call this morning." Fire Marshal Harsh told me to come to his office tomorrow morning.

In the meantime, Jun , some House of Kobe workers, Roger (my friend and my lawyer), Rick (my CPA), and John (my insurance man) came to the parking lot. "Massy, what happened?" Roger asked when he came over to me. "I don't know. I'm sure I checked all the stoves last night when I closed," I said in a daze, but I was not sure I really checked or not because every night I went through the same closing routine and it had begun to feel automatic. I did not feel like anything had been different or out of the ordinary. "What did the fire marshal say to you?" Roger asked next. "He asked me to come his office tomorrow morning," I responded. "You know, Massy, many commercial fire cases are to make an insurance claim. You might need a lawyer," he advised me. "But, Roger, unfortunately I did not take out enough insurance to cover this kind of damage," I started to explain. "Anyway, I will call you tomorrow," Roger told me before walking away and talking with a few other people. "Otosan, will we be okay? Do we have good insurance?" Jun was worried. "Hopefully okay, but I'll have to talk with John our insurance agent," I told her. The workers came over next, wanting to know, "What we should do from tomorrow?" "Don't worry. I'll make a schedule for you to work at the Frederick location," I said, trying to sound optimistic. Everything felt like I was moving in slow motion. Kenji, who by now was a sixteen year old high school student, was looking around the burned kitchen area. "Daddy, there are so many wines and beers left. Are they still useable?" he asked me. "Don't touch them, Kenji. The fire marshal is investigating how the fire started," I told him. He just kept looking around curiously.

Fire Marshal Harsh asked me a series of questions when I got to his office the following day. "Mr. Hirai, do you know what happened last night? Did you notice anything suspicious last night?" "No, it was just a normal night. I didn't pay special attention to anything and nothing seemed out of the ordinary," I responded. "Okay, I have your statement. Please do not go into the building for a while until the investigation is complete."

Next, I stopped by the insurance office. "John, will our insurance cover the costs of the fire?" I asked. "We will take care of you, but we have to wait until the investigation is over," John told me. I knew then that this would be a difficult and time-consuming issue.

A week later, I got permission from the Fire Marshal to clean up the site. So many people came to help with the clean-up. Some of them I didn't even know. Reverend Kanagy came with his friends from Bellville over an hour away. Ward's son Steve, who was the vice president of Hutzer Construction Company came with heavy dump trucks and helped remove a majority of the debris. It took more than a week to clear the site. I called the insurance agent a few more times, but he told me the same line he had when I came to his office: "we have to wait until the fire investigation is over." While we were cleaning up, Roger told me, "Massy, you should go to see my colleague, Terry Myer.

I already told him you were coming because you could be the number one suspect of this fire." "Roger, are you sure? I need a lawyer?" I asked him. I couldn't believe they'd think I would do this to my own business, one that I built from the ground up with my own hands. "Yes. You must." He was insistent. The next day, I went to Terry's office on North Potomac Street just one block away from City Hall. He asked me the almost same questions the Fire Marshal did, and told me, "Massy, you will need to go to Annapolis to take a polygraph test." "Polygraph? And go to Annapolis?" I sputtered. "Why do I need to go to Annapolis? What is the test for?" I was flabbergasted. "I'm your lawyer now. Do it for me," he answered.

Three days later, I went to take the polygraph test on the second floor of an old building located in downtown, near the Annapolis Harbor. "Mr. Hirai, Terry called me about your situation," the polygraph examiner explained. "This is a very simple test. There are 20 questions. You answer just yes, no, or I don't understand. I don't need any long answers." He explained and started to pull many wires from a machine which stood right behind me. I sat down on a comfortable armchair, and he began to attach wire sensors to my neck, heart, head, arm, legs, and hands. My heart was pounding. This seemed all very unnecessary. Then, the questions began: Do you live in Hagerstown? Are you Chinese? Did you set fire to House of Kobe restaurant? Do you have fire insurance? Are you married to a Korean woman? Do you have a girlfriend? Is your restaurant financially successful?

"Massy, we are ready against any issue that comes up," Terry said to me when I visited his office a week after I had taken the polygraph test in Annapolis. "Now, we just have to wait for Fire Marshal Harsh's decision," Terry added. For weeks, we didn't hear anything from the fire department and nothing from the insurance agent. I was worried how I'd rebuild the restaurant because I knew that even with insurance, it would cover roughly fifty percent of what I had lost. I should have chosen our insurance more carefully. Before this happened, I felt like paying for insurance was just a waste and that I'd never benefit from doling out money to insurance. Also, since we opened House of Kobe, sometimes paying the monthly premiums on time was not easy since we barely made enough to cover the overhead and employee salaries. But, it was too late to change anything now. Meantime, I would go back and forth taking care of the Frederick restaurant and waiting for news about the investigation. Fortunately, many of our customers, even those who lived in Hagerstown, would come and dine at the Frederick location.

"Massy, why don't you temporarily open House of Kobe at my place again?" Hilton offered one afternoon. "Thank you Hilton, but I don't know," I said. "Just open! I don't want to get any rent from you, so there will be no lease agreement, and all the equipment is still there. You can open from tomorrow," he urged me. I looked at him with heartfelt gratitude. He knew how difficult it had been on our family since the fire happened. "Thank you, Hilton. Really, thank you." A week after Hilton spoke with me, I opened House of Kobe at the old Dagmer Hotel. Washington County Health Department approved our permit so quickly. I couldn't believe it. It was a big help, but even still, we could not keep up monthly payments for the bank mortgage without the insurance money.

That Spring, I got an encouraging phone call. "Massy, you will be okay," Terry Myer told me confidently. "What does that mean?" I asked. "The Fire Marshal put an ad in the paper with a cash reward for information about the person that started the fire. That means they're not looking at you any longer and are trying to find the person who is guilty of arson!" Two or three weeks after the ad, the fire marshal arrested a man for arson. An old woman went to the fire department and told them, "my daughter's boyfriend set fire to that Japanese Restaurant." I attended the criminal court hearing. The arsonist was a young,

Black man who got sentenced to 26 years in the state prison. The judge asked him why he did it, and he answered, "Just for fun and show off in front of my girlfriend." I could not understand how it could be fun to set fire to someone's building? There are so many different kinds of people out there. All I knew was that I was glad my name had been cleared and we could begin re-building House of Kobe when the insurance money came through.

It felt strange starting over again but it was also a chance to make House of Kobe even better than before. Norman Morrin designed the new building which I liked, but the money from insurance wasn't enough to afford it. I would have to look for another loan. I wasn't sure if it was luck or not, but it was very timely I got financing from another bank. Cinthia Perini and Doug Metz, two of our regular customers, came to see me one day. "Massy, we would like to help you with your new House of Kobe building," Cindy told me. I had no idea they even worked at a bank. I remembered an old Japanese phrase in my mind which goes, "suteru Kami ga areba, hirou Kami mo aru." In English, it means, "There is God that loses you, but also there is God that gives you back." I went to Doug Metz' office and was so thrilled with their offer to support our new House of Kobe building renovation.

In December of 1996, House of Kobe reopened again. I invited the new Hagerstown mayor, Mayor Bruchey, and Washington County Commissioner Snook to cut the tape at our grand opening ceremony. I also invited some our regular customers to a welcome party. There was a heavy media presence; writers from the Herald Mail and Channel 25 television reporters came. We had a warm welcome and celebrated House of Kobe's new beginning.

The new design allowed us to create more space: the new dining room had ten hibachi tables, twenty regular tables, and eleven seats at the sushi bar. We also hired several more chefs to accommodate the additional tables. Both locations of House of Kobe were doing pretty well when the year 1997 began.

In March, surprisingly, I got a letter from the PGA head office saying that Seiji had been accepted into the Junior PGA series. I had forgotten that I sent an application two or three months back and was not expecting Seiji to be able to attend because he just played golf in small, local competitions. The Junior Golf Tournament would take place Saturday and Sunday two days later in Huntsville, Alabama. "Dad, I can help work at House of Kobe on Friday and Saturday night. Take Seiji to the big golf tournament. Don't worry!" Kenji told me. He was only 16 years old and in his second year at Mercersburg Academy. "Jun, you will be okay without me on the weekend?" I asked her. "Yeah, no problem. Let him try and see how he does," she responded. So, I worked Friday night until 9:00pm and Seiji and I left right afterwards. It would be about a nine-hour drive to Huntsville. Seiji's tee time was 10:30am, so we had enough time. I had already prepared a blanket and pillow for Seiji.

I was kind of excited for the trip. The route from Hagerstown to Huntsville was fairly straightforward. I would just take I-81 straight down and then change to I-75. I was so sleepy on the highway I-81 just passed the North Carolina state line, so I pulled into a service area and took a little nap. Seiji was sleeping well. I was thinking I'd take a thirty-minute nap but I ended up sleeping over two hours. I was very rushed now with time, and the morning rush hour made traffic move slowly. When we got to the Robert Trent Jones golf course, it was 10:15am. I supposed to registered 1 hours before the tee time. I quickly went to the club house, and asked one of the club pros, "Sorry we are late, but can my son still play at 10:30am?". The head club pro looked at me and said, "No problem, you're on time. You still have over an hour to wait." It was then that I realized Alabama was on Central Time rather than Eastern Time. I felt so good that Seiji's first golf tournament could start okay. I walked the car path to watch Seiji's progress along with the other parents. Seiji was cool and played well. He scored 76 on the first day. I was very tired and my legs were sore. It was my first time walking all eighteen holes on the golf course, and I had only slept those two hours in the car. After the first round, Seiji met a Black boy who was about his age at the practice area. "Kevin is deaf but is a good player. He met Tiger Woods a couple weeks ago," the boy's father told me while we were watching the boys practice together. On the second day, Seiji hit 74, and he was ranked 24th among 75 players. It was good start for his first time at a Junior golf tournament.

Since he did well, we continued to go to Junior tournaments almost every other weekend. I was very busy driving to Florida, Georgia, North and South Carolina, and Virginia as well as managing the two restaurants. Jun worked very hard, and Kenji helped almost every weekend.

In 1998, I have to give up our Frederick restaurant because another large Japanese restaurant opened near our location on West Patrick Street. The other Japanese restaurant was much more spacious, plus their location was much better, too. We lost more than 30% as soon as they opened. Because business was decreasing, the workers were no longer getting the hours they needed. We sold our business to a young Korean couple. We lost money, but I think we got out at the right time.

Kenji became a junior in high school the following fall. I took him on several college visits that year. Kenji had been always in a small, private school, so naturally he liked small colleges. The colleges he was looking into were located in Ohio, New York, Connecticut, and Massachusetts. We went to five different campuses, but he narrowed down his favorites to The College of Wooster in Ohio and Boston College in Massachusetts. I drove many miles that summertime with Kenji. During the drive, we would dream about his future together.

Kenji was excited to go back to Mercersburg Academy that fall because it was his first time living in a dormitory. I thought it was good for Kenji. He had always lived under our roof, and I thought he would learn a lot from the way that other people lived. He was doing well academically and was involved in several physically activities. His best subjects were history, math, and Latin, and he played Lacrosse well, too. I was so proud of him.

In October, one of his teachers called us with terrible news: "Kenji had a seizure during class two or three times." Jun and I realized Kenji would just stare blankly for a second or two at a time without responding to us. It wasn't happening all the time but enough to start to feel concerned. We didn't even know what the word "seizure" meant when the teacher said it, but we knew something wasn't right. After the teacher called, we took Kenji to a neurologist's office. They performed an MRI on his brain. Dr. Rosenthol gave us the results a few days after. He cleared his throat and said, "The MRI showed that Kenji has a tumor deep inside of his brain." We couldn't believe it. "I will introduce you to an excellent doctor at Johns Hopkins Hospital, and he will help Kenji," Dr. Rosenthol assured us.

A week later, we went to the new doctor's office at Johns Hopkins. There were so many people waiting for the doctor. Our appointment was for 2:30pm, but it was already 3:45 pm. I asked the people sitting around us, "our appointment is for 2:30pm. Is the wait usually this long?" A man sitting beside us nodded and said, "Usually we have to wait at least an extra hour or two. Dr. Carson is a busy doctor." A little after 4:00pm, Dr. Carson came to meet with us. He had a nice, gentle smile and a deep, soothing voice. As soon as we saw him, I already felt more comfortable.

He had this ability to make people feel calm. I forgot the frustration I had felt just moments early about waiting over two hours to see him.

Two weeks later, Kenji had brain surgery. "I removed 95% of tumor tissue, so Kenji will be okay," Dr. Carson explained. "Dr. Carson, why you could not take 100% of the tissue," I asked him. "Some of the tissue was in a sensitive area. If I took everything, Kenji would be like a vegetable. But, I believe this is not a malignant tumor, and we will give Kenji medicine that will control its growth. We will continue to check on him every month for a while, so please don't worry too much." Kenji could not go school for three weeks. His plans to go to another state for college wasn't realistic anymore since he would have to go to Johns Hopkins regularly to monitor his progress. Instead, he attended college classes at Hagerstown Junior College for a year before transferring to the University of Maryland College Park. While Kenji attended college, he did not have any more seizures and got his Bachelor's degree in four years.

Seiji still played golf in high school and became the male Maryland State High School Champion. Ashley Grier, one of Seiji's classmates at Smithsburg High School, won the women's high school championship. It was the first time both the male and female champions came from the same high school.

I was so busy with Seiji's golf and Kenji's health care. Kenji wanted to be a history teacher after college, but he started to work at House of Kobe as a full-time worker. I don't know why he changed his mind. Maybe he wanted to help me because I was so busy helping with Seiji's golf success, or maybe he enjoyed meeting people at the House of Kobe. Seiji was playing for the AJGA(American Junior Golf Association). Almost all of the PGA tour players started with the AJGA. This AJGA was a well-run organization because so many players joined. 5% of the player's tournament money went back to the AJGA as donations. So, the AJGA took care of all the young junior players and their families were treated well. Plus, sometimes, they provided free travel expenses to the top 50 players or the winner of a particular tournament. It was very special experience. I went to all the best golf courses in the US. My only regret for Seiji was I that I didn't hire a professional coach. Many of the strong junior players had their own professional coach or someone from golf school. After Seiji graduated high school, he went to Jacksonville University in Florida and played on their golf team.

On January 6th, 2002, I was driving to Dulles airport to pick up my friend Ishihara's son Hisa ,who was coming to visit us, when my cell phone rang. I had just passed Leesburg, VA. A stern voice said, "this is Immigration and Custom's Enforcement. Your illegal workers have been arrested. Please come to your restaurant as soon as possible." Suddenly, my heart started beating harder and I felt like I might get sick. When I arrived at House of Kobe, seven workers were sitting on the dining room floor. "I'm a chief of this team. Make sure they are your employees," a man in an ICE jacket barked at me. "Yes, they are my workers, and they have all ID's and have paid taxes every week," I tried to explain. "I do not know what ID they were showing you, but these are illegal workers. You have had a good reputation for a long time, so I will let you keep your business open. The federal government will send you a letter," he said in a no-nonsense tone.

I called Roger, our lawyer, who came out right away. "Massy, you've got to be careful!" Roger chided me. "Roger, I did not know so many people were working illegally because they all had ID's. So many other restaurants operate similarly." "Massy, I don't care about other restaurants. They will shut your business down next time!" he said strongly. Then, after a minute or so, he said in a calmer voice, "I'll introduce you to an immigration lawyer."

A week after, I visited the Maryland Correctional Center near Cambridge on the Eastern Shore of Maryland. I met each employee one by one separated by a glass wall and telephone. Every one of them was crying I felt so sorry for them. They were good people and hard workers. It didn't seem right that they were behind bars just for trying to make a life for their families. I felt worse when I had to tell them, "I'm sorry I can't hire you back once this is all over."

They stayed in prison three months before they were allowed to leave. Three people went back to their countries, two people moved to other states, and two came back to Hagerstown and found another place to work. I wondered how many other places of employment hired workers without papers. Three months later, I had to attend federal court in Baltimore. The female judge told me, "your restaurant has had a good reputation in Hagerstown, and since this is your first offense, I will reduce the usual penalty of $5,000 for each person, to $3,000 for each person. Since you had seven workers employed illegally, the penalty is $21,000 plus court fees of $5,000." It was a hefty fee to pay, but I learned a great lesson. I'd have to be more careful from now on.

In May 2003, Kenji graduated from University of Maryland College Park. He still graduated in four years despite his difficult health condition. For a graduation present, I thought that I might take him to Japan. "What do you think about me taking Kenji to have vacation in Japan?" I asked Jun. "That's a good idea. Kenji loves to go to Japan, and he's helped us a lot when you were away with Seiji," she pointed out. "Will you be okay to take care of the business?" I asked. "It should be fine. It's slower in the summertime," she responded.

Kenji and I went to Japan in June for two weeks. I wanted to show Japan to Kenji now that he was older. He had already been to Tokyo, Kobe, Kyoto, and Nara. I wanted to take him to the Northern Japanese city of Hokkaido, which is famous for fresh seafood, Sapporo beer, and the oldest Japanese whisky called Nikka. I knew he would enjoy it there. The first day in Japan, we stayed in Tokyo. I took him to a sushi restaurant called Edo Gin near the Tokyo Fish Market where I used to go when I was working in Tokyo. We enjoyed eating and walking the famous Ginza shopping area. As we passed a restaurant on the Ginza, I told him, "Kenji, this small sushi restaurant is very special." It was a tiny sushi bar restaurant called Jiro which had only ten seats. It is very difficult to go, I explained, because they require reservations six months in advance and costs about $500 per person to dine there. Only high-ranking government people like the Japanese Prime Minister Abe or US presidents were able to go. "Dad, why this one so expensive?" Kenji asked. "The owner, Jiro picks the best fish every morning, so when fish market closes on Sunday, Jiro restaurant is also closed too. Plus Jiro has been a famous sushi chef for a long time," I told him.

Then we rushed to the Tokyo station. As soon as we were on the platform, dark blue express train called the Cassiopeia came running in. We left Tokyo at 9:00pm and went nonstop to Sapporo in Hokkaido. We didn't get there until 9:00am the next morning. It was the first time riding the night train for both of us. Kenji was on the upper bed, and I slept on the lower bed.

It was nearly midnight, but either of us can sleep. "Kenji, you cannot sleep?" I asked. "No, Dad, I cannot sleep." "Let's go to the lounge car and have a drink," I offered. "That's a good idea.". We moved to the cocktail lounge car and sat at the bar. Kenji had Japanese whisky, and I had a beer. The view outside the train windows was almost completely dark, but sometimes we saw a grass-roofed country house near the train tracks. "Dad, I like to see old-style country houses. I don't know what it is, but they just make me warm," Kenji commented.

We had another drink and talked with the bartender. After an hour or so, we went back to bed and fell right asleep. We both woke up around 7:00am the following morning.

Sapporo is the biggest city in Hokkaido, which became even more well-known after the winter Olympics were held there in

1972. We visited the Sapporo beer factory and also visited Yoichi where the first Japanese whisky called Nikka was produced. Suntory whisky distinguished itself from Nikka after fifteen year later, and now Suntory is the one of biggest whisky companies in the world. We also went to Otaru, the oldest city in Hokkaido, and Hakodate where there are many famous seafood restaurants. It was a relaxing trip to Hokkaido. Then we went to my hometown, Kobe. We stayed with my brother in his narrow-three story house. Kenji would sometimes go out by himself to sightsee in Kobe, which has the oldest seaport in Japan. He enjoyed walking to downtown Kobe near the old embassy, which was built over 150 years ago, and he also enjoyed visiting the oldest capital, Nara. Nara was the capital almost 2000 years ago and stayed in power for 800 years. My brother Youichi would often take us to his favorite Japanese izakaya-style pub. Many Japanese pubs are very small, with only enough room for ten to twenty people and had their own specialties like chicken and fish with sake or beer. Most of the regular customers know each other and are as close as family. It was a very nice trip to Japan with Kenji. "Did you enjoy this trip to Japan?" I asked Kenji when we left Tokyo for Washington on our ANA flight. "Yes, very much!" "How did you enjoy Hokkaido?" I asked. "I liked it there, especially the seafood, but I like Kobe best" he told me. I smiled.

After Kenji came back to the US, he helped me change the House of Kobe menu. Kenji knew a lot about wine and other beverages. We made a wine menu for the first time. House of Kobe was still doing a good business in 2004 and 2005. Gradually, people became more open-minded about trying sushi because it had started to gain publicity for its health benefits. In 2006, my friend Thomas came to me and told me, "Massy, you should be careful. I heard that two or three other Japanese restaurants will open soon in Hagerstown. It might be a good idea to sell House of Kobe now. If you want, I can help you find a buyer." But, I just ignored his advice.

But it was true. There were more Japanese restaurants opening, and many grocery stores in Hagerstown began to offer sushi too. We lost a portion of business for a while, but over the months, business started increasing again. Kenji was working very hard to keep our guests happy and bring in new clientele. Seiji was still at Jacksonville University. He was still playing golf but was also enjoying college life. Since he went to college, I could not advise him anymore about balancing his golf, college life, and studying. Maki was attending the same college, and she sometimes would call me and report, "Dad, Seiji is not pay attention to his golf anymore. He drinks too much." I told Seiji, "What's going on? I heard you're not playing golf well anymore. You can enjoy college life, but not too much. Remember, this is your life." "Dad, I'm still fine. I can control myself, don't worry," he'd tell me.

Business of House of Kobe was still strong in 2007. "Otosan, I want to do something," Jun mentioned one day. "What are you thinking?" She went on. "One of my church members told me that the restaurant business is too tough, and she had a restaurant before. Now, she owns an apartment complex and enjoys her family and relaxes much more often. I found an apartment complex for sale Chambersburg. Do you think I can try?" I was surprised since this was the first time I had heard anything about her aspirations to own an apartment complex. "But you don't know anything about having an apartment business, Jun. I'm afraid you might run into a lot of trouble." "I think I can do it, don't worry. I will help you when you need money for House of Kobe. I'll be able to help," she said gently. "Let me ask Roger what he thinks. He knows a little more about this kind of thing," I told Jun. "Let me try. I know I can do it, and now Kenji works at House of Kobe, so I need to do something of my own," Jun pleaded.

When I told Roger what Jun was planning, he looked at me with a serious expression on his face. "Massy, tell Jun, don't get into this apartment business. It's a painful business." "Roger, it's too late. She's already signed the paperwork and gotten a loan approved at the bank," I said in resignation. He was right. The apartment business was tough. From the beginning, we never earned extra income. Jun asked an agent to help manage the apartments. The agent took 5% commission of all the rental income, plus they used their own company for maintenance. I had to pay extra for an apartment mortgage. In the second year, Jun canceled her contract with the agent and she was determined to maintain the apartments herself. She would go to the apartments every Saturday and clean both the interiors and exteriors, and sometimes I would have to go complete a minor repair job. Most the time, when we returned to Hagerstown, she was fast asleep in the car. When I looked at her slumped over in the passenger's side seat as we drove from Chambersburg on I-81, I couldn't believe how exhausted she looked. I had a feeling she regretted ever trying to get into this apartment business.

"Dad, how long will you keep financially supporting the apartment business?" Kenji asked me one day at House of Kobe. "I don't know how many more months, Kenji, but we cannot keep it this way for much longer." "I hope not. Business isn't as good right now as it used to be," he told me seriously. We purchased the apartments at the height of the real estate bubble in 2007. The following year, the Great Recession happened and its value plummeted. It seemed impossible to sell our apartments for a fair price. Finally, three years later, we sold the apartments for half of our original purchase price. "Sorry. I made a big mistake," Jun acknowledged when she started working at House of Kobe again. "It's okay. It's done already," I told her. The three of us, Kenji, Jun, and I, focused again on working at House of Kobe.

I became a US citizen in 2009. I was eligible for citizenship much earlier, but I did not try because I didn't want to hurt Mom's feelings. If I became a US citizen, that meant I wouldn't be a Japanese citizen any longer. But Mom turned 90 years old in 2009, so I figured that she probably wasn't concerned with my citizenship status any longer. I went to the Federal Building in Baltimore to give my testimony and received my citizenship certificate. I felt so glad to finally be an American. When I listened to national anthem, a very special, warm feeling washed over me. Jun smiled at me. She had received her citizenship four years earlier and knew how important this was to me. My hometown is now Hagerstown, MD. I have now lived here in this town longer than I lived in Japan.

In 2012, Kenji suddenly asked me if he could leave House of Kobe. "Dad, I'm ready for the challenge of another job," Kenji explained. "Why? Did you already find a job?" I asked him. "No, but I can find one." "What about your house payment? You just bought a house," I pointed out. Kenji had purchased the house only a year prior. It was a great house, and he bought at just the right time. It was foreclosed house, which were common when the recession hit, and had used Presidents Obama's first-time homebuyers' program to secure funding for it. It was located in a residential area near the Hagerstown Outlets. "Daddy, please stop Kenji from leaving." Jun's face was grave. "I can try, but I don't think he will change his mind. I think we should let him try and do what he wants to do."

Kenji had been working very hard at House of Kobe for nine years since his graduation from the University of Maryland. I also knew Kenji wanted to make a different kind of Japanese restaurant eventually, and he knew that he could not change House of Kobe. "Anyway, whatever happens, he has a place in Hagerstown," I told Jun, trying to comfort her. I felt sorry for him working House of Kobe under my management. I'm sure that Kenji was thinking about leaving House of Kobe for a long time. "Are you sure you'll be okay? Financially, I mean," I said to Kenji before he left. "Dad, don't worry. I'll be fine!" he assured me.

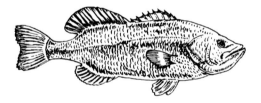

Made from Scratch: A Recipe for the American Dream

Tragedy

After three months of collecting unemployment, and he got a good job managing a restaurant called Nando's Peri Peri, which was a new global franchise that sold South African-style chicken dishes. His new position was located at their Gaithersburg Rio store. He stayed there about a year and then transferred to their Baltimore location. "Dad, I had to move to the Baltimore location which is the worst one. The head office sent me there to change some things. The location is not bad; it's between McDonalds and Panera Bread, but it needs better management," he explained on the phone. "So, you'll have to get apartment," I surmised. "What do you do about your nice house?" "My house is on the market already. I'm not worried," he answered. "Dad, it was good for me to work at House of Kobe because I think I learned a lot of things that I'll be able to use with my new job," he confided in me. "The Nando's head office is expecting me to change the Baltimore store, so it is a good challenge for me," he continued. I helped him move to his new apartment, which was only one block away from his workplace on Baltimore Street in downtown Baltimore. "Dad, I like to work for Nando's. They even cover my apartment's monthly rent. Also, I wanted to say thank you" he said quickly, handing me an envelope. There was $6,000 cash in the envelop.

"Kenji, what is all this money?" I asked incredulously. "Dad, I sold my house for a very good price. Because you made me such a nice deck, it sold more quickly and saved me a lot of money.

$6,000 is too cheap," Kenji added. I was a little sad when Kenji left from House of Kobe and worried too because he hadn't found a job yet and still had a mortgage to pay. We had been together with Kenji since he was born until he was over thirty years old. His brother Seiji and sister Maki were already married and had some kids of their own. A month later, Jun and I went to visit Kenji's place. We saw many customers next door at Panera Bread and McDonald, but Nando's was very quiet and there were only a handful of customers dining there. "Kenji, are you okay? The other restaurants are busy," I commented. "Don't worry, we'll be okay. I'm changing many things around here," Kenji smiled widely and said. "It's okay," I told Jun later, "Kenji seems very happy where he is." "Yeah, I like to see Kenji's nice smile" she agreed.

The following summer, Seiji called from North Carolina. "Dad, I am coming to back to Hagerstown." "Really?" "Joce got a new job at Frederick Community College that begins this September," he revealed. Seiji's wife, Jocelyn was a smart girl. She got her Master's degree and had a full-time job at college in North Carolina, and then later she was accepted to a doctorate program at the University Systems of Maryland. Plus, during her studies and working a full-time job, she still had and took care of their three children. Seiji was a professional golfer after college, but he later changed his permanent career to be in the food business. When they were living in North Carolina, he got a job managing an Applebee's franchise restaurant, and he enjoyed working in the food business. Anyway, it was the right time because House of Kobe needed another manager after Kenji left. I was sure Seiji would help us a lot at House of Kobe and create new Japanese dishes. Jun was very happy and was looking forward to seeing the grandchildren more often.

Christmas Day of 2013 was a memorable one. Seiji's family, Maki's family, and Kenji all came to our house. We had a big dinner and exchanged gifts with each other. They stayed from noon until nearly 8:00pm. "Dad, I'm so glad Seiji come back to Hagerstown and is helping you with House of Kobe. I was little worried because I left," Kenji said at the dinner table. "Yeah, it is good timing," I agreed. "I'm glad to work at House of Kobe. I can help you, Dad. I have many good ideas for improving business," Seiji said, and Kenji smiled and winked at me. "How is your Nando's in Baltimore?" I asked Kenji. "Dad, you wouldn't believe it! Now every lunch shift has a long line," Kenji shared proudly. I was so glad Kenji had found his spot at Nando's and seemed so excited for his future with the company. He was telling everyone that "Nando's will open in Chicago and South Dakota soon, and I may go to Chicago to help open the new store." Everyone listened to him with curiosity. "They might even expand locations in Japan, too," Kenji told me later.

One day in January 2014, Kenji called while I was getting ready to open House of Kobe for the day. "I'm sorry, Dad. I have bad news… my brain tumor has come back again." "Don't be sorry Kenji. I thought you checked on things every six months. Did something happen?" I asked. "I did not check the past two years because I thought everything was okay. I did not have any seizures or anything! But, last week, I had an awful headache and vision problems, so I went to the doctor's office right away. He sent me to Johns Hopkins right away as soon as he saw my health history. I got the results of my MRI today," he said, trying to put on a brave voice. "Mom and I will go to the hospital with you," I told him.

"How are you? I'm Dr. Winegart," said a tall man with a friendly face as he walked into the room. We tried to stand up, but he gestured for us to sit down. "I know Kenji," he came out and said straight away. We looked at each other with curiosity, trying to place how he would have known Kenji. "Actually, I was a surgeon fifteen years ago, and Dr. Carson was my mentor," he said. As soon as he explained that he remembered Kenji, we felt so much better. "I know what he need to be done. Please don't worry too much. Surgery will be a day after tomorrow, and it will probably be about a four or five hour surgery. Kenji will stay overnight at the hospital, so we can make sure he begins to recover well." As we received more information about the surgery and process for recovery, we began to feel better. "Kenji, it is good that Dr. Winegart remembered you," Jun said when we left. I could tell she was trying to make him feel less anxious about the upcoming surgery.

Kenji went to operation room at 7:00am the following day, and at 1:00pm, we still hadn't heard any news. Jun and I were staying in the fifth floor waiting room at Johns Hopkins Hospital. I kept checking the surgery information board every few moments, but Kenji's number still read "in surgery." Jun went to the information desk asking about Kenji's situation many times, but the old woman who was at the receptionist desk didn't have anything to report. Trying to pass the time, we just looked at the tall buildings around us and the cargo ships that were coming in and out of the harbor area in Baltimore. Maki and Seiji called two or three times to check on Kenji's progress. After what felt like forever, I finally saw Kenji's status read "recovering room" around 6:00 pm, nearly 11 hours after they wheeled him into surgery. The waiting room receptionist came to us said kindly, "please go to the meeting room down the hall. Dr. Winegart will be there waiting for you." Jun and I looked at one another. Usually, the doctors would come to waiting area right after the surgery if there was good news, but he wanted to see us in a meeting room. We were so worried because 11 hours in surgery was much longer than they told us it would be. When we arrived at the meeting room, Dr. Winegart came in right away. "I'm sorry it took so long. Kenji has a malignant tumor. I took 93% of the impacted tissue out. Let's wait two weeks for him to heal, and then I recommend having radiation treatment and chemotherapy treatment," he advised. I froze during his explanation. "You can wait for Kenji to wake up and then go in and see him," he added. We wanted to ask the doctor so many questions, but no words came to our lips. We were just shocked at the news that the tumor was malignant.

A little while later, we were allowed to see Kenji. I was little afraid to speak in case his head was throbbing, but I couldn't help but ask, "Kenji, are you okay?" Kenji couldn't speak but looked at me and opened his eyes a bit more widely, signaling that he was okay. His face was bruised and swollen. Jun and I told him over and over, "I love you Kenji." Each time, he responded with his eyes. Jun was openly crying, and I was crying on the inside. Jun wanted to stay with Kenji overnight. I left the hospital around 9:00pm for Hagerstown to close House of Kobe and came back early the next morning.

Kenji's color was better than the previous day. "Dad, Kenji slept pretty good, but I didn't sleep much, Jun told me quietly. Then, Kenji spoke. "The doctor told me I have stage 4 cancer." "Dr. Winegart told us the tumor was malignant, but he did not tell us it was stage 4," I said, surprised. "He told me this morning." I looked at Kenji, who was trying to stay so strong and positive. He stayed at the hospital another two days before going back to his apartment in Baltimore. Jun and I switched off days staying at Kenji's apartment with him for the next week. He appeared to be recovering well. Two weeks later, we visited Dr. Winegart's office as part of a routine check-up after surgery. As soon as the doctor removed the gauze from Kenji's head, his face turned grim and he checked his watch. "Kenji's incision has become infected. He's going to need another surgery, but it's too late to start today. We'll keep him overnight and go into surgery at 7:00am," he announced. Kenji looked at Jun and I as if to say, "not again."

The next day, Kenji had another brain surgery. Jun and I spent another anxious day on the fifth floor waiting room. Dr. Gordon, another one of Kenji's doctors, came to the waiting room around 1pm. "We've cleaned all the bad tissue out. Kenji will be fine," he told us right away, sensing our concern. He added, "Kenji will stay here overnight, and please go to Dr. Winegart's office tomorrow morning. He will give you instructions for the antibiotic injections. Dr. Winegart gave us the injectable medications the following morning at his office with the following instructions:"Mr. Hirai, please stay with Kenji for a month. He will need someone to help him with the injection every eight hours."

For the next month, I stayed with him every day. Sometimes, Jun would come stay too. But Kenji seemed more comfortable with me there. He had to keep the tube for the injection clean and dry all the time, even when taking showers. It was very hard for the first week, but he could handle it more easily the second and third week after his surgery. I could leave him for short periods of time after week three. He was getting stronger all the time. Sometimes, we go to restaurants together in the evening. He had lived in Baltimore only six month, but he already knew pretty much all the good places to go in downtown Baltimore. We stopped almost every morning at the Lexington Market for donuts. Kenji loved to chat with the old, Jewish couple that owned the donut shop. I think these outings perked his spirits up.

A month later, he was infection free. He started radiation treatment for six weeks followed by chemotherapy treatment for another six weeks. They put him on a heavy dose of steroid medications during his course of chemotherapy. Kenji's weight quickly went from 170 lbs. to 260 lbs., which I know was hard on him. I was always busy, going to Kenji's apartment, taking him back and forth from Johns Hopkins three days a week, and taking care of the business in Hagerstown. Seiji began to manage House of Kobe around this time, which allowed me to spend more time with Kenji. It was an especially difficult year.

Kenji missed working at Nando's. Nando's' Baltimore got a new manager named Tracey from the head office in Washington, DC. Whenever I'd stop in, she would exclaim, "Mr. Hirai, Kenji did a great job managing this place. Can you see how busy this restaurant is now?" "You know Kenji? He loved working her," I'd tell her.

We tried just about everything to help Kenji's condition. Jun had the idea to try Eastern medicine. "Dad, I heard old Korean herbs can help shrink cancer cells. One of my church members told me." So we ordered a special combination of herbs from Korea. There was a strong, pungent smell that would take over the whole house because we have had to cook them slowly over low heat. "Mom, I don't want to take this one," Kenji asserted. "I know it is stinky but it might help you," Jun tried to encourage him. "I'm not going to take this. It's not going to help me," he argued. "Kenji, just try it for me," I asked him later when we are alone. "Okay, I'll take it this time, but please don't order it anymore," he finally agreed. He begrudgingly took this herb mixture for the next six months. In the summer of 2015, Kenji had moved back into our house from his apartment in Baltimore. He just needed more care, and this way, either Jun or I could be with him all the time. In addition to the herbs Jun was giving him, Kenji still underwent chemotherapy treatments at the oncology department of Johns Hopkins Hospital once a week.

After Thanksgiving, Kenji fell unconscious. I took him to the emergency room at Johns Hopkins. We found out Kenji had a stroke caused by the tumor, which had started growing again. The next day, he had a third brain surgery to relieve some of the pressure the tumor was causing. But after surgery, the right side of his body was paralyzed. He came back home after two weeks of rehabilitation treatments in the hospital. Jun was pushing him to get acupuncture after he got home, but Kenji was again resistant. "Dad, I know one very good acupuncture doctor in Virginia," Jun had shared with me before we took him home from the hospital. "But, I'm sure Kenji does not want to try acupuncture. He doesn't believe in that kind of thing," I told her. "Can you push him? We've got nothing lose now. Let's just try," Jun pleaded. When I had the chance, I spoke to Kenji at Jun's request. "Kenji," I started, "in the old days back in Japan and Korea, acupuncture was a very popular treatment for its ability to fix and heal. Of course, nothing will happen quickly, but it might improve your blood circulation and make you feel better." "Dad, I don't believe in that, and I don't want to," Kenji refused. "Just do it for me." He did not say anything right away, and a while later he conceded again. "Okay, I'll try, but on one condition. You have to take me back to Japan when I get better." Kenji grinned.

From there on out, every day was filled. I'd take Kenji every Wednesday and Saturday for acupuncture in Annandale, Virginia. Every Tuesday I'd take him to oncology appointments with Dr. Grossman at Johns Hopkins. Every Thursday, he had rehabilitation appointments at the medical campus in Hagerstown. Kenji did not like to go to acupuncture for the first few weeks, but he gradually began to relax as the acupuncturist filled his body with thin needles. "Mr. Hirai, I think Kenji enjoys coming here now because he most of the time he is sleeping," Dr. Yin told me. During his acupuncture treatment , I would go sit in a nearby coffee shop and read a book or browse the internet. When the hour was up, I'd go back to the doctor's office, push his wheelchair to the car, open the passenger's side door, and help move Kenji from the wheelchair to the car seat. "Dad, thank you. The coffee smells good," he'd say. I always got a coffee for Kenji to sip on the way back to Hagerstown. Kenji liked listening to music, and I usually tried to put on his favorite songs by artist Billy Joel. Sometimes, when he was up to it, we'd stop by the Nando's store in Gaithersburg and take chicken wraps to-go. This was our routine. Kenji tried very hard to keep a positive mindset. He hated using the wheelchair and tried to learn to walk with a cane instead. About this time, I started sleeping in Kenji's room just in case he would lose his footing when he'd get up and go to the bathroom in the middle of the night. Kenji and I were together most of the time. Sometimes, we'd talk, and sometimes we'd just sit quietly and watch the tv. Other times, we'd have a drink of red wine and listen to jazz out on the back porch. He loved to drink wine and would savor each sip. I think it helped him feel more normal to enjoy the things he loved. He never talked about his future anymore, though. We kept conversation light and stuck to topics like history and Japanese foods.

By 2016, his new MRI's showed that the tumor was growing again. It was an aggressive tumor and Kenji was fighting hard. Kenji had his fourth brain surgery, radiation, and another round of chemotherapy treatment. We spoke with Dr. Grossman, who was the director of the oncology department at the hospital.

"Dr. Grossman, is there any other medicine that can help Kenji? There are so many medicine companies coming out with experimental treatments" I asked after we exhausted all the other options. "Mr. Hirai, yes. There are many cancer medications out there, but cancer is very difficult because there are so many different types of cancer cells," he explained. "We can look into getting a new medication that just came out, but the insurance company won't cover it. The medication would be $25,000 for a 30 day supply," Dr. Grossman shared.

A week later, Dr. Grossman called. "Mr. Hirai, I have a good news. Kenji will take that new medicine. I already talked with the insurance company, and they will cover the cost if Kenji participates in a study at Johns Hopkins." "Yes, that's great. Thank you very much, Dr. Grossman," I said gratefully. "Mr. Hirai, remember, there is no guarantee this will work. All we can do is hope that it will help Kenji," Dr. Grossman reminded me.

We got a special delivery two weeks later from the pharmaceutical company. It was big storage box filled with dry ice. We were so happy to get news at the end of 2016. It was the first time that the tumor stopped growing since Kenji found out about the tumor in 2014. Yes, the new medicine was helping . Kenji take MRI check every month. 20% tumor shrink in January. 50% tumor shrink in February. 70% tumor shrink in March.

In March 2017, I got a telephone call from Japan. It was my brother. "Aniki, Mother is not good in condition. Can you come to Japan?" "Is this a serious situation? "I asked. "I don't know, but she is 95 years old," he said sternly. I decide to go to visit Kobe since Kenji's situation was a little better. "Kenji, do you think you can go to Japan with me?" I asked hopefully. "Dad, you know I'd love to go, but I should wait a little longer," he responded. I know that Kenji loved Mima and wished he could be there, so I visited Japan for a week. When I went to Mom's hospital, she saw me and called out "Kenji." "She confused Aniki with Kenji because she took care of Kenji when he was born," brother tried to explain. My mother's condition had declined considerably since I saw her last, but she was stable for the entire week that I was there. "How was Mima?"Kenji asked me when I came back a week later. "She is still hanging on, but she kept calling me Kenji all week," I shared with him. Kenji just laughed.

While I continued to stay with Kenji, Seiji was working on a new menu and making some minor renovations to the hibachi section at House of Kobe. In April, after Kenji took another MRI, we headed to Dr. Grossman's office to get the results. "Kenji, good news today, " Dr. Grossman said. "There's only 10% of tumor left, and I'd like to have your permission to publish your health record because this is a real miracle medicine," Dr. Grossman's partner, Dr. Schrick asked. Kenji smiled when he heard the word miracle and said, "Yes, of course" to Dr. Schrick. "There is another person that's taking this medicine, too." "How is that person doing?" Kenji asked. "She is fine too, just like you," Dr. Schrick said with wonder. Another MRI wasn't due until the following May, three months later.

That May, Kenji took another MRI. As we were walking to Dr. Grossman's office, he nudged me. "Dad. If I get good result today, I want to go Japan with you this summer." "Yeah, we should go. Mima will be very happy to see you," I agreed. Soon, Dr. Grossman and Dr. Schrick came while we were still talking about Japan. Dr. Grossman looked pained as he told us, "Kenji, I don't have good news. The MRI showed that a new tumor has grown by 20%." "Dr. Grossman, I don't understand. Back in January, the tumor had shrunk so much. I was expecting Kenji to be cancer free today," I told him. "Mr. Hirai, cancer is very difficult. We don't know exactly how or why this can occur, but the medication killed one area of malignancy while another one grew. I'll have to talk with Dr. Winegart tomorrow about the best way to move forward for Kenji." Kenji and I left feeling discouraged when we left Johns Hopkins. We were just both quiet the whole ride back to Hagerstown. I was sure that Kenji was thinking about what had just happened, but I just had no words. I called Jun about how the appointment went when I went to the bathroom. Like Kenji and I, she was saddened by the news. "I had hoped to plan a surprise celebration dinner for tonight when we learned that Kenji was cancer free," she revealed. "Dad, don't worry. I'll just keep fighting. Did you tell Mom?" Kenji told me when we pulled up to the house on Harp Road. "Yeah, she knows." Jun was waiting outside for us. As soon as he opened the door, she just hugged him tightly.

Kenji had brain surgery a week later, his fifth. Once he recovered, we went back to our routine: acupuncture every Wednesday and Saturday and going to Johns Hopkins for chemotherapy every Tuesday again. I don't know how, but Kenji's mind was still positive. I still slept in Kenji's room every night. I sleep on the floor, and Kenji slept in his bed. One night, I heard a noise and opened my eyes. Kenji was sitting on his bed and looking at me. I almost woke up, but I did not because I saw Kenji's hands wiping his eyes. He was crying. I just ignored it and pretended to be asleep. I wanted to hug him and cry together, but I did not. I thought if he saw me crying that he'd be even more sad. About ten minutes later, he laid back down. I didn't sleep the rest of the night. "Dad," Kenji called down to me at about 7:00am. He tried to sound normal, but his voice was still thick. He seemed to feel a little better after that, turning on some good music in the car and talking about House of Kobe on the way to Baltimore that day.

In June 2017, Jun called one night when I was working at House of Kobe. Her voice sounded panicked. "Daddy, can you come home? Kenji is in a lot of pain." "Did you give him aspirin?" "Of course, but nothing is helping." I left the restaurant right away. When I got home, Kenji's face was pale. "I'll take him to the emergency room," I told her. We headed straight for Johns Hopkins. It was Friday night, and the hospital was very busy. Kenji was still hanging on. An hour later, we were taken to a room and waited for the doctor. "Please bring a comfortable chair for my dad," Kenji asked the nurse. "Don't worry about me. I'm okay," I said to Kenji. I was almost crying. There is was no comparison between my sleepiness and Kenji's immense pain. When they took him for an x-ray, I just kept thinking about how thoughtful Kenji was.

The doctor came a short while after Kenji returned from the x-ray. He explained, "Kenji's stomach and intestines have small holes in them, and there's liquid in his lungs. We will need to surgery quickly." No wonder Kenji was in so much pain. "I recommend talking with your oncology doctor. Kenji may have another issue," the emergency room doctor added. Kenji could not go home from that point on and stayed at Johns Hopkins

Hospital. He had to have a feeding tube put in and a tracheostomy to help him breathe.

"Kenji, today is your birthday, but I can't take you anywhere today. We'll all go to the Bahamas for next your birthday, okay?" Jun whispered to him. Kenji couldn't speak but just looked into her eyes. His health was declining rapidly, and they moved him to the ICU. He passed away on July 20th, 2017, at 5:30pm. He lived only 36 years and 12 days. Kenji was the finest man in the world.

✦✦✦

Kenji's funeral was held at Hagerstown Nazarene Church on July 24th, 2017, a Monday. Kenji didn't go to church, but he liked Pastor Johnson. We did not announce the funeral publicly, yet 500 people attended. House of Kobe was closed on Monday, but we hosted all of Kenji's friends for dinner in his memory. The doctors from Johns Hopkins Hospital and people from Nando's Peri Peri head office and stores also attended the funeral and dinner afterward. Kenji touched so many people's lives. Jun and I were physically and mentally drained. It had only been three weeks since we rushed Kenji to the emergency room that one last time. I felt like all this had been a dream, that I'd soon wake up and Kenji would be right there again.

Seiji took on more hours at House of Kobe especially from July 20th, 2017. Fortunately, the business was strong and we were gaining new customers in addition to the loyal base that we had. We kept Kenji's room exactly the way he left it because we felt Kenji's presence still there. I could still smell him and hear his voice. It was a very difficult first Christmas without Kenji. All the workers at House of Kobe usually had a Christmas party on Saturday night a week before December 25th, but we did not have the party in 2017.

Slowly, the year passed. The following summer, we threw a memorial party in Kenji's honor. I invited all Kenji's friends, more than 100 people. Somebody told me "sorry, but the passing of time will help," but I didn't think the year without him had helped anything. I did not see any clear, nice skies since July 2017.

In 2018 and 2019, Maki started to work at House of Kobe two or three days a week. It seems she enjoyed working at House of Kobe. I had more time to take care of things I neglected when Kenji was ill, like cleaning our yard, fixing broken things around the house, and taking care of our farm property in Boonsboro. I enjoyed being busy because as soon as I'd sit down, all I would think about is Kenji. He was constantly on my mind. When I was driving, I'd always think about him. We had spent so much time together in the car those last few years, drinking coffee and listening to music. The conversations we had would re-play in my mind. "Dad, I like this street, Oak Hill Avenue. There are nice, old houses and tall maple trees on the side of each street. Hagerstown used to be an important city on the East Coast, did you know that?" Kenji loved to talk about history. So when I'd pass by Oak Hill Avenue, it felt like Kenji was still there beside me in the passenger's seat.

I couldn't be too sad, especially in front of Seiji and Maki. They are very special children, too. Fortunately, Seiji and Maki have been able to help grow the business at House of Kobe. But soon, I have to decide what the future will be for House of Kobe. Seiji likes the restaurant business and has good skills for handing the daily operations. But, Seiji and Maki cannot work together. They are both such independent people. Plus, Seiji wants to have a small izakaya-style restaurant of his own someday. Maybe I'll have to keep operating the business of House of Kobe until I take my last breath.

CORONA

In early 2020, the world was struck down by the Covid-19 pandemic. We had to close the business for two weeks and only offer take-out for the following month. We lost so many workers. Somehow, throughout this period, business was strong. Our customers were loyal and kept coming despite the strangeness of the world around us. Other businesses were being shuttered all around us due to severe worker shortages or Covid outbreaks. The federal government began to send out stimulus checks to help improve the economy during the massive shutdown, which helped people afford to continue supporting businesses like ours, but workers also did not have as much incentive to come to work when they got this financial support.

House of Kobe celebrated its 40th anniversary in 2021. I was hoping to have a party in November, but a winter surge of Covid made it too dangerous. Yet, I have much to celebrate. In 1974, one tiny seed was planted in American soil, and 43 years later that seed became a huge tree with many branches and strong roots. I met so many people who taught me, helped me, and loved me. I have a wonderful family of eleven, including five beautiful grandchildren. My journey has almost reached its final destination. I am proud of myself.

✦✦✦

Sunday October 17, 2021.

I drove to our Boonsboro farm for my 75th birthday party. Many people attended this party. Three weeks before the party, Maki told me "Daddy, I want to have big party for your 75th birthday." I said, "no, I don't need one." I wasn't really interested in having a party. There were two reasons I wasn't comfortable. One reason, of course, was the Covid situation, which was still a concern after two years. The other reason was that I just didn't feel like it was necessary to have a big party. However, Jun, Seiji, and Maki felt that a 75th birthday is very special. They all agreed that an "outside party should be much safe than indoors." I gave them the go-ahead with only three weeks to prepare. Maki, Seiji, and Jun quickly prepared the event. They did a marvelous job. They transformed the farm with decorated dinner tables and a tent with a DJ, Fireworks, and tables upon tables of tasty foods the workers at House of Kobe had all prepared. So many people came and celebrated my birthday. It was my happiest memory since Kenji left us.

After the party for my 75th, I have been thinking more deeply about the life I've lived and how everything turned out. It's been almost 50 years since I've lived in the United States, nearly twice as long as I lived in Japan. I have lived through so many challenges and turning points. It seems to be that I was walking wrong road because of working at the farm and home as a house boy and college student long time. But at the same time I met many special people ,and had very special opportunity. And I learn so many things for the life.

I had a dream when I was just a kid living in Japan: *I will go to America and work very hard. I'll build my own house myself since it is almost impossible to build own house myself in Japan due to the lack of land. Once I do this, I'll take all my favorite items and put them on a sailboat and came back to Japan. I'll live on the northern part of the countryside near the ocean, sit by the sea, watch the waves, and think about how life was.*

I changed my dream when I had my first child, Kenji. I remember thinking: *This baby is from me.* I watched his face and touched his hands and legs for a long time. *Yes, Kenji is my baby and I have to take care of him and make our family. If I work hard, I can make my children's future bright.* This is all I wanted. Fortunately, life granted me three wonderful children.

The restaurant business is always challenging. I always felt sorry for my children Jun or I could not take off every weekend, couldn't sit together at the dinner table, and most of the time, the children already sleep when I came home. Yet, I was glad that we could go on three or four vacations every year. I took them to Japan and other US vacation places like Miami, Boca Raton, Orlando, Hilton Head, the Bahamas, Homestead, Martha's Vineyard, New York City, Niagara Falls. I wanted them to see other parts of the world.

I'm so appreciative all our family helped with House of Kobe. All three children understood that our situation was different from other families and they all still grew up so nicely. I am so proud of my children. I am especially proud Kenji lived on so strongly in the face of his situation. He never lost hope and continued to think about others even when fighting for his life. I've accepted his early departure, and even though I still miss him deeply, I did not want him to continue living in pain and suffering. He gave me so many memories that I cherish and will never forget. I am also very lucky that Maki and Seiji made such wonderful families. I have lived to see the 2nd and 3rd generation of the Hirai family are strongly rooted into American soil.

We spent a great Thanksgiving Day at Seiji's house in 2021. I remember my first Thanksgiving Day in 1974 at the Ikard's residence in Shepherdstown. I helped Mr. Ikard prepare a big dinner for his own family from early in the morning. He made both a ham and turkey. It was very cold day. All their children were coming from Texas, and I thought it was such a lovely tradition for all their family to get together and enjoy a meal. It was good to see everyone laughing and enjoying one' another's company.

But I had the toughest time. I was not expecting to have dinner with them at the table, but it was so depressing to eat a meal myself in the corner of their kitchen. I almost gave up on living in the US so many times. I remember how I could have stayed in Japan or stayed in Hawaii and not come to Washington, DC at all. I was very strong, stubborn person. Maybe that was okay because I never gave up. 48 years after that first lonely Thanksgiving meal, I sat down to eat a good meal with my own family and watched everyone enjoy eating and talking together. How different life is now. I am the luckiest person in the world.

Dear Kenji,

This is my story. I am sorry that I could not completed before your departure. However, I believe you see everything from the sky. What do you think about my journey? I hope you enjoy reading this story. I can hear your voice "Dad! You have very interesting life, I am very proud of you".

Thank you Kenji.!

I think that you are the key person to give strength in the family and business House of Kobe, and also give to me life is so interesting and wonderful.

Thank you Kenji to be my son

Made from Scratch: A Recipe for the American Dream

Application

Thank you very much to:

Jocelyn for nice editing.

Ryan for good art work.

John at HBP.

This wonderful book could not exist without above persons.

I also thank you to:

Maki and Ryan, Jocelyn and Seiji are taking care of families very well with 5 great grandchildren. This is my real Dream which my 3 generation strongly stand up on American soil.

And thank you to my wife Jun.

✦ ✦ ✦